# EASY PORTUGUESE PHRASE BOOK

## Over 1500 Common Phrases
## For Everyday Use And Travel

www.LingoMastery.com

# Free Book Reveals the 6-Step Blueprint That Took Students **from Language Learners to Fluent in 3 Months**

- **6 Unbelievable Hacks** that will accelerate your learning curve

- **Mind Training:** why memorizing vocabulary is easy

- **One Hack to Rule Them All:** This secret nugget will blow you away...

Head over to **LingoMastery.com/hacks**
and claim your free book now!

# CONTENTS

# INTRODUCTION

Brazil is usually known for its friendly and cheerful people, natural diversity, soccer, good music and, of course, the Carnival! Surely, there is much to explore and enjoy while traveling in this South American country but, although Brazilians are used to receiving many tourists and are welcoming with guests, most natives either do not speak a foreign language or might feel quite shy to have a conversation in English. This language barrier may become even more challenging if the chosen place is a picturesque destination, such as an indigenous village in the middle of the Amazon rainforest or a small beach in Bahia (a beautiful northeast state).

Thanks to this book, we will see how to deal with many situations that can be simple, complicated, funny, or even not funny at all – all those real situations that a tourist will experience when, for example, they seek activities to do, order a perfectly cooked *feijoada* in a restaurant, or simply do not want to be bothered. Think of the souvenirs to bring back to a relative. Do you want to negotiate on the price or ask for a discount? We can help you with all of that!

Speaking in the native language during a trip demonstrates that you respect their culture and that you strive to communicate correctly. Besides gaining the sympathy of Brazilians - which will make your trip way more pleasant, you may be surprised by unexpected discounts, extra tips or even new friends, since good communication can really open doors. Most of the time, a translation with the vocabulary at your fingertips is the best solution, and therefore, why not take precautions and study a few phrases that could amaze your fellow travelers or your interlocutors?

Of course, there are some obstacles to overcome. Take, for example, the challenges that can create difficulties at a phonetic level in the Brazilian Portuguese language.

# Pronunciation of Brazilian Portuguese vowels

Although the vowels of Brazilian Portuguese have the same written form as in English (the letters A, E, I, O, U), there are important differences when it comes to pronunciation, especially because Portuguese tends to be a very nasal language. Phonetically speaking, in Brazilian Portuguese there are eight oral vowels (open and close) and five nasal vowels, which we will see below, according to each letter.

## The vowel A

The most common and general sound of this vowel is the open A, just like the way you pronounce it in 'father'.

Abacaxi (pineapple), *ah-bah-kah-SHEE*
*// the letter X has multiple sounds in Portuguese. In this case, it sounds like –sh, as in 'she'.*

Árvore (tree), *ÁR-voe-ree*
*// the 'A' sound is the same here; the function of the acute accent is to indicate the stressed syllable. So just remember that if you ever see an acute accent, the sound is the same as in 'bar'.*

Bola (ball), *BOH-lah*
*// regardless of the position in the word, the A is still pronounced like in 'car'!*

Barato (cheap), *bah-RAH-too*
*// the R has also multiple sounds in Brazilian Portuguese. Here, it would be like the way Americans would pronounce the double 't' in 'better'. Do not worry though – we will learn about that later.*

Amor (love), *Ah-MOR*
*// good word to practice, huh?*

The second and last way to pronounce the A is the nasal sound. It should be similar to the nasal sounds of 'sun', 'want' or 'country'. You will be able to know that the A has a nasal sound when it is positioned before the letter N; when you see the grapheme *tilde* (~) above it; or when you see a circumflex accent (^) above it.

Ambos (both) *AM-boos*

Copacabana (the famous beach in Rio de Janeiro) *co-pa-ca-BAHN-na*
Manhã (morning) *man-GNAN*
Ângulo (angle) *AHN-goo-loo*
Ansioso (anxious), *ahn-see-OE-soo*.

## The vowel E

There are three different sounds for this vowel: the open, the close and the nasal 'E'.

The open 'E' is pronounced similarly to the 'e' to be found in the English words 'get' or 'set'. It does not necessarily need to have any marker, but in some cases, there might be an acute accent to indicate the stressed syllable.

Festa (party) *FEHS-tah*
Café (coffee) *kah-FEH*
Janela (window) *zha-NEH-la*
Pé (foot) *peh*
Meta (goal) *MEH-ta*

The second way to pronounce the 'E' is the close sound. It is not very common to have this sound in English, but it is similar to the 'e' to be found in the English words 'they' and 'grey' – try to focus on the 'e', ignoring the 'y', though. This sound can be found in the ordinary 'e' of when it has the circumflex accent (^).

Ser (to be) *sayh*
Dedo (finger) *DAY-doo*
Gelo (ice) *ZHAY-loo*
Por quê? (why?) *pooh-KAY*
Medo (fear) *MAY-doo*

Finally, the third sound of 'E' has the famous nasal sound. As it happens with the vowel 'A', you know you should pronounce it nasal when it appears before 'N' – and in the case of this vowel, also 'M'. This sound is quite close to the English sound of 'em' in 'emphasis'.

Dentro (inside) *DAYN-troo*
Quem (who) *kayn*
Também (also) *tam-BAYN*
Tempo (time) *TAYM-poo*
Fazenda (farm) *fah-ZAYN-da*

*// Important note: every time this vowel appears at the end of a word and there is no acute or circumflex accent, it should sound like 'ee'. E.g. pele (skin) PEH-lee; leite (milk) LAY-chee*

## The vowel I

Here, we can use the same pattern as we learned with 'A': there is a standard sound (which might have the acute accent to indicate the stressed syllable or not) and the nasal sound.

By the way, pay attention to the fact that, in English, this vowel might have multiple sounds, while in Portuguese, the standard 'I' is only pronounced as its English pronunciation in 'ski'.

Item (item) *EE-tayn*
Fica (he/she stays) *FEE-ka*
País (country) *pah-EES*
Pia (sink) *PEE-ah*
Igreja (church) *ee-GRAY-zha*

Now, let's see some examples of the nasal sound of 'I'. We can pronounce it similar to the English pronunciation of 'been', 'green' or 'seem', but try to focus on the vowel sound, ignoring the 'n' or 'm' sounds. It is also possible that this vowel has an acute accent, but unlike the case of 'A', there is no circumflex accent.

Sim (yes) *seem*
Símbolo (symbol) *SEEM-boe-loo*
Biquini (bikini) *bee-KEEN-nee*
Cinto (belt) *SEEN-too*
Simples (simple) *SEEM-plees*

## The vowel O

For comparison purposes, 'O' works pretty similar to 'E': there are the open, the close and the nasal sounds.

The open sound might have an acute accent or not and is pronounced similarly as the 'o' in the English word 'core'.

Porta (door) *POHR-ta*
Óbvio (obvious) *OH-bee-vyo*

Avó (grandmother) *ah-VOH*
Famosa (famous –fem.) *fa-MOH-za*
Óculos (glasses) *OH-coo-loos*

The close sound of 'O' is very similar to the 'o' pronounced in the word 'go', but a little bit softer. It might have a circumflex accent or not – remember that the reason for it to appear is a certain need to indicate the stressed syllable.

Boca (mouth) *BOE-ka*
Avô (grandfather) *ah-VOE*
Bolo (cake) *BOE-loo*
Fogo (fire) *FOE-goo*
Ovo (egg) *OE-voo*

*// Important note: every time the vowel 'O' appears at the end of a word and there is no acute or circumflex accent, it should sound like 'oo', as we can see in the last three examples above.*

Referring to the nasal sound of 'O', we can recognize it when it comes before 'M' or 'N'. Say it as the English speakers say the word 'own'.

Ombro (shoulder) *OWN-broo*
Ontem (yesterday) *OWN-tayn*
Ônibus (bus) *OWN-nee-boos*
Sombra (shadow) *SOWN-bra*
Bom (good) *BOWN*

## The vowel U

Finally, we can understand the use of this vowel in the same way as the use of 'A' and 'I': there is the standard sound and the nasal sound (when it comes before 'm' or 'n').

The standard 'U' is quite similar to the English pronunciation of 'oo' in 'food'.

Pulga (flea) *POO-ga*
Uva (grape) *OO-vah*
Luta (fight) *LOO-ta*
Maduro (mature) *ma-DOO-roo*
Útero (uterus) *OO-tay-roo*

In its turn, the nasal sound of 'U' is similar to the English pronunciation of 'oo' in 'room' or 'moon'.

Um (one) *oom*
Alguns (some) *ahw-GOON-s*
Nunca (never) *NOON-ka*
Mundo (world) *MOON-doo*
Atum (tuna) *ah-TOOM*

## 'W' and 'Y'

For a long time, these letters (also including 'K') were not officially recognized as part of the Portuguese alphabet – they were considered as "foreign letters", because they were only utilized in international proper names or brands. However, thanks to Globalization and the increasing addition of international words to the Portuguese vocabulary, K, W and Y are now considered as part of the alphabet. The sound of 'Y' is equivalent to the sound of 'I'. W, in its turn, has the standard sound of 'U', but for same names (especially German proper names) it could also be read as 'V'. Consequently, 'W' is considered as a vowel if it sounds like 'U' or as a consonant if it sounds like 'V'. Look at some examples below:

Kiwi (kiwi fruit) *kee-WEE*
Show (concert) *identical pronunciation as in English*
Wagner (proper name) *VAHG-neh*
Wesley (proper name) *WEHS-lay*
Trobogy (a neighborhood in Salvador) *troe-boe-ZHEE*
Yasmim (proper name) *yas-MEEM*

## Pronunciation of Vowel Combinations in Brazilian Portuguese

There are quite a few ways of combining vowels in the Brazilian Portuguese language. At first, we call the combination of two vowels in the same syllable a diphthong and the combination of three vowels a triphthong. For a combination of two vowels in different syllables, we call it a hiatus.

## Diphthongs

The diphthongs are divided into falling and rising.

Falling diphthongs begin with a vowel of high pitch and end with a semivowel of less prominence, as it happens to the English word 'eye'.

Leite (milk) *LAY-chee*
Oito (eight) *OEY-too*
Papel (paper) *pah-PEHW*

On the other hand, rising diphthongs start with a semivowel and end with a more prominent vowel, similar to what happens in 'yard'.

Quase (almost) *KWAH-zee*
Farmácia (drugstore) *far-MAH-seea*
Quando (when) *KWAN-doo*

## Hiatus

Remember that a hiatus happens when two vowels appear together in a word but belong to different syllables. One example in English could be the word 'reenter'.

Piada (joke) *pee-AH-da*
Moeda (coin) *mo-EH-da*
Lua (moon) *LOO-a*

## Triphthongs

A triphthong is always formed by three vowels that appear together and belong to the same syllable. In addition, they always follow the same order: semivowel + vowel + semivowel. A simple example in English would be the word 'hour'.

Igual (same) *EE-guaw*
Qualquer (any) *kwaw-KEHH*
Ninguém (nobody) *neen-GAYN*

# Portuguese consonants

## Similar consonants in Brazilian Portuguese and English

Several consonants that, in general, are used in Brazilian Portuguese pretty much the same way as you would use them in English. This applies to: **b, c, f, g, k, l, m, n, p, q, v.**

Anyway, some of them deserve further considerations:

**C**: it works exactly the same way as in English, with its rules and exceptions.

When it comes before A, O or U, it sounds like 'K', like in 'car', 'copy' and 'Cuba'.

> Casa (house) *KAH-za*
> Curitiba (a big city in South Brazil) *koo-ree-CHEE-ba*

If it comes before E or I, it will sound like 'S', like in 'cell' and 'cinnamon'.

> Celular (mobile phone) *say-LOO-lah*
> Cinto (belt) *SEEN-too*

And now we bring you a peculiarity: in Portuguese, 'C' may also appear like 'Ç'. It is called *cedilla*, which is not considered a letter, yet a mark. It can only be used before A, O and U, and it will always sound like 'S'.

> Cachaça (a sugarcane liquor) *kah-SHAH-sa*
> Almoço (lunch) *ahw-MOE-soo*
> Açúcar (sugar) *ah-SOO-kah*

**G**: this letter also obeys the rule of changing its pronunciation depending on the vowel that comes after it. Having said that, when G comes before 'E' or 'I', it is pronounced differently than the way it is usually pronounced in English. Try to say it always as the sound of 'G' in 'beige'.

> Gelo (ice) *ZHAY-loo*
> Girassol (sunflower) *zhee-rah-SOHW*
> Viagem (trip) *vy-AH-zhayn*

**L**: when it appears before a vowel, it is just like in English. However, in Brazilian Portuguese when the L is located at the end of a syllable, it should sound like 'U'.

Sal (salt) *sahw*
Hotel (hotel) *oe-TEHW*
Calma (calm) *KAW-ma*

**M**: if this letter appears before a vowel, it works exactly the same as in English. However, when the 'M' appears at the end of a syllable (and this happens quite often in Portuguese), such syllables should be pronounced as a nasal sound and the 'M' should not be pronounced – that is, you should not touch your lips.

Sim (yes) *seem*
Bom (good) *bown*
Bem (well) *behm*

**Q**: as you may have noticed, in English there is always a 'U' after this consonant, which is not different in Portuguese. However, you need to know that sometimes the 'U' will not be pronounced, so the 'Q' will sound like 'K'.

Quero (I want) *KEH-roo*
Quintal (backyard) *keen-TAHW*
Queijo (cheese) *KAY-zhoo*

The only way for you to know when the 'U' should be pronounced or not is by practice. Do not worry, though. We will show you the most important words and its pronunciation throughout this phrasebook.

## Brazilian Portuguese consonants that work differently than in English

Good news: Although these consonants are pronounced in a different way than in English, all sounds that will be presented below are already known by English speakers. Let's start with some pairs:

## D and T

When you find these consonants before A, O or U, the pronunciation is pretty much similar to the English one – just watch that it will sound more like a native speaker if you put your tongue right in the middle of your teeth.

On the other hand, when these letters are found before E or I (and only when both sound like 'ee'), then a phenomenon called *palatalization* happens. It is not rocket science, you can just say it like 'jeep' for D, and 'cheese' for T.

Dia (day) *GEE-ahh*

Tarde (afternoon) *TAR-gee*

Tomate (tomato) *to-MAH-chee*

## S and Z

We know that, in English, each one of these consonants have their own sounds. However, in Portuguese there are some simple rules:

When the 'S' is found between two vowels, it necessarily sounds like a 'Z'. When it is not, it sounds normally like 'S'.

Casa (house) *KAH-za*
Sorriso (smile) *soe-HEE-zoo*
Gostar (to like) *goes-TAR*

In its turn, Z will always sound like 'Z', except when it is found at the end of a syllable. In this case, it will sound like 'S'.

Paz (peace) *PA-ys*
Voz (voice) *VOH-ys*
Zoológico (zoo) *zoe-oe-LOH-zhee-koo*

*// Important note: everytime there is an 'S' or 'Z' at the end of a word (which happens a lot in plural words), Brazilians tend to include the 'ee' sound before those letters. E.g. gás (gas) GAH-ees; luz (light) LOO-ees. Speaking this way will make you sound way more natural and clear.*

## R

The rule for this letter is quite similar to the one used for 'S'. Its standard sound is like the 'H' in English, such as 'hi' or 'hair'. However, when it appears between two vowels, it changes to a sound like the 'T' in 'better' (North American accent).

Rua (street) *HOO-a*
Barato (cheap) *bah-RAH-too*
Marido (husband) *mah-RI-doo*

## H

Pretty simple: in Brazilian Portuguese, it is always mute.

Hora (hour) *OH-ra*
História (History) *ees-TOH-ree-a*
Hábito (habit) *AH-bee-too*

## J

Here, there is no variation either. The only way to pronounce the 'J' in Portuguese is like the sound of 'G' in 'beige'.

Jovem (young) *ZHOH-vain*
Já (already) *zha*
Beijo (kiss) *BAY-zhoo*

## X

At last, the only consonant that has four possible sounds: the X. There is no rule to help us identify when to pronounce it the proper way, just practicing it. Yes, that scares Brazilians too!

The 'X' can sound like 'sh' in 'shave'.

Xarope (syrup) *sha-ROH-pee*
Lixo (trash) *LEE-shoo*

It can sound like 'S' in 'some'.

Próximo (next) *PROH-see-moo*
Texto (text) *TAYS-too*

The 'X' can also sound like 'Z' in 'zebra'.

Êxito (success) *AY-zee-too*
Exemplo (example) *ay-ZAIN-ploo*

Finally it can sound like 'KS', as in 'taxi'.

Complexo (complex) *kom-PLEH-ksoo*
Tóxico (toxic) *TOH-ksy-koo*

## Combined consonants in Brazilian Portuguese

In this session, we are going to clarify objectively the correct pronunciation of each digraph, that is, when two letters represent only one sound. Most of them exist in English, but the first two are more *exotic*.

## LH

This could be a little bit harder, but not that much. It sounds similar to the doubled 'L' sound in 'million'.

Milho (corn) *MEE-lyu*
Palhaço (clown) *pah-LYAH-soo*

## NH

Say it just like you say the 'gn' part in 'lasagna'.

Amanhã (tomorrow) *ah-man-GNAN*
Vizinho (neighbor) *vee-zee-GNYU*

## CH

This is an easy one. Whenever you find it, just pronounce it 'sh', as in 'she'.

Chuva (rain) *SHOO-va*
Cachorro (dog) *ka-SHOE-hoo*

## RR

The doubled 'R' is always pronounced like the 'H' of 'hi'.

Carro (car) *KA-hoo*
Churrasco (barbecue) *shoo-HAHS-koo*

## SS, SC, SÇ and XC

All of these combinations represent the sound of 'S'. Easy, right?

Pássaro (bird) *PAH-sa-roo*
Descer (to go down) *day-SAYH*
Cresço (I grow up) *CRAY-soo*
Excelente (excellent) *ay-say-LAIN-chee*

## GU and QU

In both these combinations, the 'U' can be pronounced or not – and that is a matter of use, we have no rule for that.

Água (water) *AH-gwa*
Preguiça (laziness) *pray-GHEE-sa*
Cinquenta (fifty) *seen-KWAIN-ta*
Esquerda (left side) *ees-KAYR-da*

## Bonus notes on Brazilian dialects

Brazil is definitely a multicultural country. Throughout its history, the nation has received millions of immigrants from many countries, such as Italy, Germany, Japan, Lebanon, Nigeria, Ghana, and many. After all this mix of cultures and languages, it is expected to find multiple dialects in Brazil.

Depending on the dialect, some sounds presented above may vary. There are three main variations that are worth mentioning:

**D and T**: in most parts of the Brazilian northeast, there is no palatalization of these letters before the 'I' sound. Therefore, they are pronounced similarly to the way one would pronounce in English.

Dieta (diet) *gee-EH-ta or dee-EH-ta*.

**R**: this one may sound like the 'H' in 'hi', the 'tt' in 'better' (North American accent) or even the ordinary 'R' that English speakers are used to pronounce!

Carne (meat) *KAHH-nee or KAR-nee or KARRR-nee*.

**S**: depending on the region, at the end of a syllable this letter may sound like an ordinary 'S', as used in English, or like 'sh' in 'show'.

Escolas (schools) *ees-KOH-las or eesh-KOH-lash*

For standardization purposes, in this book we will use the dialect used in Brasília, the capital city, where locals are considered as having "no accent". As that city has been constructed only 60 years ago and its locals have come from all parts of Brazil, this is certainly a good standard for us to use.

# A note about the Brazilian way of addressing people

As in most countries, Brazilians tend to be formal in some contexts, like at work, at school or when talking to the elderly. In this case, it is considered polite and respectful to use the reference 'o senhor' (sir) *oo-saign-OH* for men and 'a senhora' (lady) *ah-saign-OTTA* for women.

"O senhor sabe onde é a praia?" (Do you know where the beach is?) *oo-saign-OH SAH-by OWN-gee EH ah PRAh-ya?*
"A senhora vende bolo?" (Do you sell cakes?) *ah-saign-OTTA VAIN-gee BOH-loo?*

When talking in an informal context, however, we can use 'você' (you) *voh-SEH*.

"Você é daqui?" (Are you from here?) *voh-SEH EH da-KEE?*

Important note: when talking to a young person in the street, use 'você', regardless if that person is a stranger. Use 'o senhor' and 'a senhora' exclusively to talk to the elderly.

# A gendered language

Just like other Latin languages, Portuguese is a gendered language, that is, some words are considered as *feminine* and other words are considered as *masculine*. Most of the time, the feminine words end with '-a' and the masculine words end with '-o'. Anyway, in this phrasebook we will make it clear for you when a word has both a feminine and a masculine version, so you can choose the one that fits the idea you want to express.

# COLORS

**Gold**
Dourado (masc.),
dourada (fem.)
*doe-RAH-doo (masc.),
doe-RAH-da (fem.)*

**Red**
Vermelho (masc.),
vermelha (fem.)
*vayr-MAY-lyu (masc.),
vayr-MAY-lya (fem.)*

**Orange**
Laranja
*lah-RAN-zha*

**Yellow**
Amarelo (masc.),
amarela (fem.)
*ah-mah-REH-loo
(masc.), ah-mah-REH-
la (fem.)*

**Green**
Verde
*VAYR-gee*

**Blue**
Azul
*ah-ZOO*

**Light blue**
Azul claro
*ah-ZOO CLAH-roo*

**Violet**
Violeta
*vee-oe-LAY-ta*

**Pink**
Rosa
*HOH-sa*

**Brown**
Marrom
*mah-HOM*

**Purple**
Roxo (masc.), roxa
(fem.)
*HOE-shoo (masc.),
HOE-sha (fem.)*

**White**
Branco (masc.),
branca (fem.)
*BRAN-koo (masc.),
BRAN-ka (fem.)*

**Black**
Preto (masc.), preta
(fem.)
*PRAY-too (masc.),
PRAY-ta (fem.)*

**Gray**
Cinza
*SEEN-za*

**Silver**
Prata
*PRA-ta*

**What color is that sign?**
De que cor é esse sinal?
*gee kee koeh eh AY-sy see-NAW?*

**Is the cartoon in color?**
O desenho animado é em cores?
*oo day-ZAYN-gnoo ah-nee-MAH-doo eh ayn KOE-rys?*

**Is this television show in color?**
Esse programa de TV é em cores?
*AY-sy proe-GRAM-ma gee tay-VAY eh ayn KOE-rys?*

**This is a red pen.**
Essa é uma caneta vermelha.
*EH-sa eh OO-ma kan-NAY-ta vayr-MAY-lya.*

**This piece of paper is blue.**
Esse pedaço de papel é azul.
*AY-sy pay-DAH-soo gee pah-PEHW eh ah-ZOO.*

**What color is that car?**
De que cor é esse carro?
*gee kee koeh eh AY-sy KAH-hoo?*

**What color are your clothes?**
De que cor é a sua roupa?
*gee kee koeh eh ah SOO-a HOE-pa?*

**Is this the right color?**
Essa é a cor certa?
*EH-sa eh ah kor SEH-ta?*

**What color is the stop light?**
De que cor é esse semáforo?
*gee kee koeh eh AY-sy say-MAH-foe-roo?*

**Does that color mean danger?**
Essa cor significa perigo?
*EH-sa koeh seeg-nee-FEE-ka pay-REE-goo?*

**That bird is red.**
Esse passarinho é vermelho.
*AY-sy pah-sah-REEN-nyu eh vayr-MAY-lyu.*

**What color is that animal?**
De que cor é aquele animal?
*gee kee koeh eh ah-KAY-ly ah-nee-MAH-oo?*

**The sky is blue.**
O céu é azul.
*oo SAY-oo eh ah-ZOO.*

**The clouds are white.**
As nuvens são brancas.
*ahs NOO-vains sawm BRAN-kas.*

**That paint is blue.**
Essa pintura é azul.
*EH-sa peen-TOO-rah eh ah-ZOO.*

**Press the red button.**
Aperte o botão vermelho.
*ah-PEHH-chee oo boe-TAUM vayr-MAY-lyu.*

**Don't press the red button.**
Não aperte o botão vermelho.
*NANN-oo ah-PEHH-chee oo boe-TAUM vayr-MAY-lyu.*

**Black and White**
Preto e branco
*PRAY-too y BRAN-koo*

**Look at all the colors.**
Olhe para todas as cores.
*OH-lye PAH-ra TOE-das ahs KOE-rys.*

**Is that a color television?**
Isso é uma TV em cores?
*EE-soo eh OO-ma tay-VAY ayn KOE-rys?*

**What color do you see?**
Que cor você está vendo?
*Kee kor voe-SAY ees-TA VAIN-doo?*

**Can I have the color blue?**
Pode ser na cor azul?
*POH-gee sayh nah koeh ah-ZOO?*

**What colors do you have for these frames?**
Quais cores você tem para esses quadros?
*KWA-ees KOE-rys voe-SAY tayn PAH-ra AY-sys KWA-droos?*

**Don't go until the color is green.**
Não vá até que a luz fique verde.
*NANN-oo vah ah-TEH kee ah loos FEE-ky VAYR-gee.*

**Colored pencils**
Lápis de cor
*LAH-pees gee koeh*

**Coloring pens**
Canetas de colorir
*kan-NAY-tas gee koe-loe-REEH*

**The sharpie is black.**
O apontador é preto.
*oo ah-pon-ta-DOEH eh PRAY-too*

**Do you have this in another color?**
Você tem isso em outra cor?
*voe-SAY tayn EE-soo ayn OE-tra koeh?*

**Do you have this in a darker color?**
Você tem isso numa cor mais escura?
*voe-SAY tayn EE-soo NOO-ma koh MAH-ees ays-KOO-ra?*

**Do you have this in a lighter color?**
Você tem isso numa cor mais clara?
*voe-SAY tayn EE-soo NOO-ma koh MAH-ees KLAH-ra?*

**Can you paint my house blue?**
Você pode pintar minha casa de azul?
*voe-SAY POH-gee peen-TAR MEE-nya KAH-za gee ah-ZOO?*

**Can you paint my car the same color?**
Você pode pintar o meu carro da mesma cor?
*voe-SAY POH-gee peen-TAH oo MAY-oo KAH-hoo dah MAYZ-ma koeh?*

**The flag has three different colors.**
A bandeira tem três cores diferentes.
*Ah ban-DAY-ra tayn trays KOE-rys gee-fay-RAIN-chees.*

**Is the color on the flag red?**
A cor da bandeira é vermelha?
*ah koeh dah ban-DAY-ra eh vayr-MAY-lya?*

# NUMBERS

**Zero**
Zero
*ZEH-roo*

**One**
Um
*oom*

**Two**
Dois (masc.); duas
(fem.)
*doys (masc.); DOO-as
(fem.)*

**Three**
Três
*trays*

**Four**
Quatro
*KWA-tro*

**Five**
Cinco
*SEEN-ko*

**Six**
Seis
*SAY-s*

**Seven**
Sete
*SEH-chee*

**Eight**
Oito
*OEY-too*

**Nine**
Nove
*NOH-vy*

**Ten**
Dez
*DEH-ys*

**Eleven**
Onze
*OWN-zee*

**Twelve**
Doze
*DOE-zee*

**Thirteen**
Treze
*TRAY-zee*

**Fourteen**
Quatorze
*ka-TOEH-zee*

**Fifteen**
Quinze
*KEEN-zee*

**Sixteen**
Dezesseis
*gee-zay-SAY-s*

**Seventeen**
Dezessete
*gee-zay-SEH-chee*

**Eighteen**
Dezoito
*gee-ZOEY-too*

**Nineteen**
Dezenove
*gee-zay-NOH-vy*

**Twenty**
Vinte
*VEEN-chee*

**Twenty-one**
Vinte e um
*VEEN-chee y oom*

**Twenty-two**
Vinte e dois
*VEEN-chee y doys*

**Twenty-three**
Vinte e três
*VEEN-chee y trays*

**Twenty-four**
Vinte e quatro
*VEEN-chee y KWA-tro*

**Twenty-five**
Vinte e cinco
*VEEN-chee y SEEN-ko*

**Twenty-six**
Vinte e seis
*VEEN-chee y SAY-s*

**Twenty-seven**
Vinte e sete
*VEEN-chee y SEH-chee*

**Twenty-eight**
Vinte e oito
*VEEN-chee y OEY-too*

**Twenty-nine**
Vinte e nove
*VEEN-chee y NOH-vy*

**Thirty**
Trinta
*TREEN-ta*

**Forty**
Quarenta
*kwa-RAIN-ta*

**Fifty**
Cinquenta
*syn-KWAIN-ta*

**Sixty**
Sessenta
*says-SAIN-ta*

**Seventy**
Setenta
*say-TAYN-ta*

**Eighty**
*Oitenta*
*oy-TAYN-ta*

**Ninety**
Noventa
*noe-VAIN-ta*

**One hundred**
Cem
*sain*

**Two hundred**
Duzentos
*doo-ZAIN-toos*

**Five hundred**
Quinhentos
*keen-NYEN-toos*

**One thousand**
Mil
*myw*

**One hundred thousand**
Cem mil
*sain myw*

**One million**
Um milhão
*oom my-LYAUM*

**One billion**
Um bilhão
*oom bee-LYAUM*

**What does that add up to?**
Quanto dá tudo?
*KWAN-too dah TOO-doo?*

**What number is on this paper?**
Qual número está nesse papel?
*kwaw NOO-may-roo ees-TAH NAY-sy pah-PEHW?*

**What number is on this sign?**
Qual número está nessa placa?
*Kwaw NOO-may-roo ees-TAH NEH-sa PLAH-ka?*

**Are these two numbers equal?**
Esses dois números são iguais?
*AY-sys doys NOO-may-roos sawm ee-GWAYS?*

**My social security number is one, two, three, four, five.**
Meu número de previdência social é um, dois, três, quatro, cinco.
*MAY-oo NOO-may-roo gee pray-vee-DAYN-sya eh doys, trays, KWA-tro, SEEN-ko.*

20

**I'm going to bet five hundred euros.**
Vou apostar quinhentos euros.
*voe ah-poes-TAH keen-GNAIN-toos EW-roos.*

**Can you count to one hundred for me?**
Você pode contar pra mim até cem?
*voe-SAY POH-gee kon-TAR prah meem ah-TEH sain?*

**I took fourteen steps.**
Dei quatorze passos.
*day ka-TOR-zee PAH-soos.*

**I ran two kilometers.**
Corri dois quilômetros.
*KOE-hee doys ky-LOE-may-troos.*

**The speed limit is 30 km/h.**
O limite de velocidade é 30 km/h.
*oo lee-MEE-chee gee vay-lo-see-DAH-gee eh TREEN-ta ky-LOE-may-troos poeh OH-ra.*

**What are the measurements?**
Quais são as medidas?
*KWA-ees sawm ahs may-GEE-das?*

**Can you dial this number?**
Você pode discar para este número?
*voe-SAY POH-gee GEES-kah PAHra AYS-tee NOO-may-roo?*

**One dozen.**
Uma dúzia.
*OO-ma DOO-zya.*

**A half-dozen.**
Meia dúzia.
*MAY-ah DOO-zya.*

**How many digits are in the number?**
Quantos dígitos tem no número?
*KWAN-toos GEE-zhy-toos tayn noo NOO-may-roo?*

**My phone number is nine, eight, five, six, two, one, eight, seven, eight, eight.**

O número do meu telefone é nove, oito, cinco, seis, dois, um, oito, sete, oito, oito.

*oo NOO-may-roo doo MAY-oo tay-lay-FOE-nee eh NOH-vy, OEY-too, SEEN-ko, SAY-s, doys, oom, OEY-to, SEH-chee, OEY-too, OEY-too.*

**The hotel's phone number is one, eight hundred, three, two, three, five, seven, five, five.**

O telefone do hotel é um, oitocentos, três, dois, três, cinco, sete, cinco, cinco.

*oo tay-lay-FOE-nee doo oe-TEHW eh oom, oey-too-SAYN-toos, trays, doys, trays, SEEN-ko, SEH-chee, SEEN-ko, SEEN-ko.*

**The taxi number is six, eight, one, four, four, four, five, eight, one, nine.**

O número do táxi é seis, oito, um, quatro, quatro, quatro, cinco, oito, um, nove.

*oo NOO-may-roo doo TAK-sy eh SAY-s, OEY-too, oom, KWA-tro, KWA-tro, KWA-tro, SEEN-ko, OEY-to, oom, NOH-vy.*

**Call my hotel at two, one, four, seven, one, two, nine, five, seven, six.**

Ligue para o meu hotel: dois, um, quatro, sete, um, dois, nove, cinco, sete, seis.

*LEE-ghee PAH-ra oo MAY-oo oe-TEHW: doys, oom, KWA-tro, SEH-chee, oom, doys, NOH-vy, SEEN-ko, SEH-chee, SAY-s.*

**Call the embassy at nine, eight, nine, eight, four, three, two, one, seven, one.**

Ligue para a embaixada: nove, oito, nove, oito, quatro, três, dois, um, sete, um.

*LEE-ghee PAH-ra ah aim-bye-SHA-da: NOH-vy, OEY-too, NOH-vy, OEY-too, KWA-tro, trays, doys, oom, SEH-chee, oom.*

# GREETINGS

**Hi!**
Oi!
*OE-y!*

**How's it going?**
Como vai?
*KOE-moo VA-ee?*

**What's new?**
Quais são as novidades?
*KWA-ees sawm ahs noe-vee-DAH-gees?*

**What's going on?**
O que tem feito?
*oo kee tayn FAY-too?*

**Home, sweet home.**
Lar, doce lar.
*lah, DOE-see lah.*

**Ladies and gentlemen, thank you for coming.**
Senhoras e senhores, obrigado por terem vindo.
*saying-OH-ras ee saying-OH-rees, oe-bree-GAH-doo poeh TAY-rain VEEN-doo.*

**How is everything?**
Tudo bem?
*TOO-doo bayn?*

**Long time, no see.**
Há quanto tempo.
*ah KWAN-too TAYM-poo.*

**It's been a long time.**
Faz tempo que não nos vimos.
*FAH-ees TAYM-poo kee NANN-oo noos VEE-moos.*

23

**It's been a while!**
Faz algum tempo que não nos vimos.
*FAH-ees ahw-GOOM TAYM-poo kee NANN-oo noos VEE-moos.*

**How is life?**
Como anda a vida?
*KOE-moo AN-da ah VEE-da?*

**How is your day?**
Como está o seu dia?
*KOE-moo ees-TAH oo SELL GEE-ahh?*

**Good morning.**
Bom dia.
*bown GEE-ah.*

**It's been too long!**
Faz muito tempo!
*FAH-ees MOON-ee-too TAYM-poo!*

**Good afternoon.**
Boa tarde.
*BOE-a TAR-gee.*

**How long has it been?**
Faz quanto tempo?
*FAH-ees KWAN-too TAYM-poo?*

**It's a pleasure to meet you.**
É um prazer te conhecer.
*eh oom pra-ZAYR chee koe-GNAY-sayh.*

**It's always a pleasure to see you.**
É sempre um prazer ver você.
*Eh SAYN-pree oom prah-ZAYR vayr voe-SAY.*

**Allow me to introduce Earl, my husband.**
Deixa eu apresentar Earl, meu marido.
*DAY-sha AY-oo ah-pray-zain-TAH Earl, MAY-oo mah-REE-doo.*

**Goodnight.**
Boa noite.
*BOE-a NOY-chee.*

**May I introduce my brother and sister?**
Posso apresentar os meus irmãos?
*POH-soo ah-pray-zain-TAH oos MAY-oos eer-MAWNS?*

**Good evening.**
Boa noite.
*BOE-a NOY-chee.*

**What's happening?**
O que está acontecendo?
*oo kee ees-TAH ah-kon-tay-SAIN-doo?*

**Happy holidays!**
Boas festas!
*BOE-as FEHS-tas!*

**Are you alright?**
Está tudo bem com você?
*Ees-TAH TOO-doo bayn kom voe-SAY?*

**Merry Christmas!**
Feliz Natal!
*fay-LEES nah-TAW!*

**Where have you been hiding?**
Onde você esteve se escondendo?
*OWN-gee voe-SAY STAY-vee see ays-kon-DAIN-doo?*

**Happy New Year!**
Feliz Ano Novo!

*fay-LEES ANN-noo NOE-voo!*

**How is your night?**
Como está a sua noite?

*KOE-moo ees-TAH ah SOO-a NOY-chee?*

**What have you been up to all these years?**
O que você tem feito todos esses anos?
*oo kee voe-SAY tayn FAY-too TOE-doos AY-sysANN-noos?*

**When was the last time we saw each other?**
Quando foi a última vez que nos vimos?
*KWAN-doo foy ah OO-chee-ma vays kee noos VEE-mos?*

**It's been ages since I've seen you.**
Não te vejo há séculos.
*NANN-oo chee VAY-zhoo ah SEH-koo-loos.*

**How have things been going since I saw you last?**
Como as coisas estão indo desde que nos vimos?
*KOE-moo as KOY-zas ees-TAWM EEN-doo DAYS-dee kee noos VEE-moos?*

**What have you been up to?**
Quais são as novidades?
*KWA-ees sawm ahs noe-vee-DAH-gees?*

**How are you doing?**
Como você tá?
*KOE-moo voe-SAY tah?*

**Goodbye.**
Tchau.
*CHAH-oo.*

**Are you okay?**
Você está bem?
*voe-SAY ees-TAH bayn?*

**How's life been treating you?**
Como a vida está te tratando?
*KOE-moo ah VEE-da ees-TAH chee tra-TAN-doo?*

**I'm sorry.**
Sinto muito.
*SEEN-too MOON-ee-too.*

**Excuse me.**
Com licença.
*Kom lee-SAIN-sa.*

**See you later!**
Até mais tarde!
*ah-TEH MAH-ees TAR-gee!*

**What's your name?**
Qual é o seu nome?
*Kwaw eh oo SAY-oo NOE-me?*

**My name is Bill.**
O meu nome é Bill.
*oo MAY-oo NOE-me eh Bill.*

**Pleased to meet you.**
É um prazer te conhecer.
*eh oom prah-ZAIR chee koe-GNAY-sayh.*

**How do you do?**
Como vai?
*KOE-moo VA-ee?*

**How are things?**
Como estão as coisas?
*KOE-moo ees-TAWM as KOY-zas?*

**You're welcome.**
De nada.
*gee NAH-da.*

**It's good to see you.**
Que bom te ver.
*kee bown chee vayh.*

**How have you been?**
Como você está?
*KOE-moo voe-SAY ees-TAH?*

**Nice to meet you.**
É um prazer te conhecer.
*Eh oom prah-ZAYR chee koh-NAY-say.*

**Fine, thanks. And you?**
Estou bem, obrigado. E você?
*IS-toe bayn, oe-bree-GAH-doo. y voe-SAY?*

**Good day to you.**
Um bom dia pra você.
*oom bown GEE-ah prah voe-SAY.*

**Come in, the door is open.**
Entra, a porta tá aberta.
*AIN-tra, ah POHR-ta ees-TAH ah-BEHR-ta.*

**My wife's name is Sheila.**
O nome da minha esposa é Sheila.
*oo NOE-me dah MEE-nya ees-POE-za eh Sheila.*

**I've been looking for you!**
Eu tava te procurando!
*EH-oo TAH-va chee proe-koo-RAN-doo!*

**Allow me to introduce myself. My name is Earl.**
Deixa eu me apresentar. O meu nome é Earl.
*DAY-sha AY-oo mee ah-pray-zain-TAH. oo MAY-oo NOE-me eh Earl.*

**I hope you have enjoyed your weekend!**
Espero que você tenha curtido o final de semana!
*Ays-PEH-roo kee voe-SAY TAYN-gna koor-CHEE-doo oo fy-NAW gee say-MANN-na!*

**It's great to hear from you.**
Que ótimo receber notícias suas.
*kee OH-chee-moo hay-say-BAYH noe-CHEE-syas SOO-as.*

**I hope you are having a great day.**
Espero que você esteja tendo um ótimo dia.
*Ays-PEH-roo kee voe-SAY ays-TAY-jah TAYN-doo oom OH-chee-moo GEE-ah.*

**Thank you for your help.**
Obrigado pela ajuda.

*oe-bree-GAH-doo PAY-la ah-ZHOO-da.*

# DATE AND TIME

**January**
Janeiro
*zhan-NAY-roo*

**February**
Fevereiro
*fay-vay-RAY-roo*

**March**
Março
*MAH-soo*

**April**
Abril
*ah-BREEW*

**May**
Maio
*MAH-yu*

**June**
Junho
*ZHOO-nyu*

**July**
Julho
*ZHOO-lyu*

**August**
Agosto
*ah-GOES-too*

**September**
Setembro
*say-TAYN-bro*

**October**
Outubro
*oe-TOO-broo*

**November**
Novembro
*noe-VAIN-bro*

**December**
Dezembro
*day-ZAIN-broo*

**What month is it?**
Estamos em qual mês?
*ees-TAM-moos ayn kwaw MAY-s?*

**At what time?**
Que horas?
*kee OH-ras?*

**Do you observe Daylight saving time?**
Vocês têm horário de verão?
*voe-SAYS tayn oe-RAH-ryo gee vay-RAUM?*

**The current month is January.**
Estamos no mês de janeiro.
*ees-TAM-moos noo MAY-s gee zhan-NAY-roo.*

**What day of the week is it?**
Que dia da semana é hoje?
*kee GEE-ah da say-MANN-na eh OE-zhee?*

29

**Is today Tuesday?**
Hoje é terça?
*OE-zhee eh TAYH-sa?*

**Today is Monday.**
Hoje é segunda.
*OE-zhee eh say-GOON-da.*

**Is this the month of January?**
Estamos em janeiro?
*ees-TAM-moos ain zhan-NAY-roo?*

**It is five minutes past one.**
É uma hora e cinco minutos.
*eh OO-ma OH-ra y SEEN-ko my-NOO-toos.*

**It is ten minutes past one.**
É uma hora e dez minutos.
*eh OO-ma OH-ra y DEH-ys my-NOO-toos.*

**It is ten till one.**
São dez pra uma.
*sawm DEH-ys prah OO-ma.*

**It is half past one.**
É uma e meia.

*eh OO-ma y MAY-ah.*

**What time is it?**
Que horas são?
*kee OH-ras sawm?*

**When does the sun go down?**
Quando o sol se põe?
*KWAN-doo oo SOH-w see PONN-ee?*

**It's the third of November.**
É três de novembro.
*eh trays gee noe-VAIN-bro.*

**When does it get dark?**
Quando começa a escurecer?
*KWAN-doo koe-MEH-sa ah ays-koo-ray-SAYH?*

**What is today's date?**
Qual é a data de hoje?
*kwaw eh ah DAH-ta gee OE-zhee?*

**What time does the shoe store open?**
Que horas abre a loja de sapatos?
*kee OH-ras AH-bree ah LOH-zha?*

**Is today a holiday?**
Hoje é feriado?
*OE-zhee eh fay-ree-AH-doo?*

**When is the next holiday?**
Quando vai ser o próximo feriado?
*KWAN-doo VAH-ee sayh oo PROH-see-moo fay-ree-AH-doo?*

**I will meet you at noon.**
Vou te encontrar ao meio-dia.
*voe chee ain-kon-TRAH AH-oo MAY-oo GEE-ahh.*

**I will meet you later tonight.**
Vou te encontrar hoje à noite.
*voe chee ain-kon-TRAH OE-zhee ah NOY-chee.*

**My appointment is in ten minutes.**
O meu compromisso é em dez minutos.
*oo MAY-oo kom-pro-MEE-soo eh ayn DEH-ys my-NOO-toos.*

**Can we meet in half an hour?**
A gente pode se encontrar daqui a meia hora?
*ah ZHAIN-chee POH-gee see ain-kon-TRAH dah-KEE ah MAY-ah OH-ra?*

**I will see you in March.**
Te vejo em março.
*chee VAY-zhoo ayn MAH-soo.*

**The meeting is scheduled for the twelfth.**
O encontro está marcado para o dia doze.
*oo ain-KON-troo ees-TAH mah-KA-doo PAH-ra oo GEE-ah DOE-zee.*

**Can we set up the meeting for noon tomorrow?**
Podemos deixar a reunião pro meio-dia de amanhã?
*po-DAY-moos day-SHAR ah ray-oo-nee-AUM PAH-ra MAY-oo GEE-ahh gee ah-man-GNAN?*

**What time will the cab arrive?**
Que horas o táxi vai chegar?
*kee OH-ras oo TAK-sy VAH-ee shay-GAH?*

**Can you be here by midnight?**
Você pode chegar aqui antes da meia-noite?
*voe-SAY POH-gee shay-GAH ah-KEE AN-chees da MAY-ah NOY-chee?*

**The grand opening is scheduled for three o'clock.**
A grande abertura está marcada para as três horas.
*ah GRAN-gee ah-bayh-TOO-ra ees-TAH mah-KA-da PAH-ra ahs trays OH-ras.*

**When is your birthday?**
Quando é o seu aniversário?
*KWAN-doo eh oo SAY-oo ah-nee-vayh-SAH-ryu?*

**My birthday is on the second of June.**
O meu aniversário é em dois de junho.
*oo MAY-oo ah-nee-vayh-SAH-ryu eh ayn doys gee ZHOO-nyo.*

**This place opens at ten a.m.**
Esse lugar abre às dez da manhã.
*AY-sy loo-GAR AH-bree ahs DEH-ys dah man-GNAN.*

**From what time?**
A partir de que horas?
*ah pah-CHEEH gee kee OH-ras?*

**Sorry, it is already too late at night.**
Desculpa, já é muito tarde da noite.
*gees-KOO-pa, zha eh MOON-ee-too TAR-gee dah NOY-chee.*
Common Questions

**Do you speak English?**
Você fala inglês?

*voe-SAY FAH-la een-GLAYS?*

**What is your hobby?**
Qual é o seu hobby?
*Kwaw eh oo SAY-oo hobby?*

**What language do you speak?**
Qual idioma você fala?
*kwaw ee-gee-OE-ma voe-SAY FAH-la?*

**Was it hard?**
Foi difícil?
*foy gy-FEE-seew?*

**Can you help me?**
Você me ajuda?
*Voe-SAY mee ah-ZHOO-da?*

**Where can I find help?**
Onde eu posso encontrar ajuda?
*OWN-gee AY-oo POH-soo ain-kon-TRAH ah-ZHOO-da?*

**Where are we right now?**
Onde estamos agora?
*OWN-gee ees-TAM-moos ah-GOH-ra?*

**Where were you last night?**
Onde você estava ontem à noite?
*OWN-gee voe-SAY ees-TAH-va OWN-tayn ah NOY-chee?*

**What type of a tree is that?**
Que tipo de árvore é essa?
*kee CHEE-poo gee AH-voe-ree eh EH-sa?*

**Do you plan on coming back here again?**
Você pensa em voltar aqui de novo?
*voe-SAY PAIN-sa ayn voe-TAH ah-KEE gee NOE-voo?*

**What kind of an animal is that?**
Que animal é esse?
*kee ah-nee-MAHW eh AY-sy?*

**Is that animal dangerous?**
Esse animal é perigoso?
*AY-sy ah-nee-MAHW eh pay-ree-GOE-zoo?*

**Is it available?**
Está disponível?
*ees-TAH gees-poe-NEE-vew?*

**Can we come see it?**
A gente pode ir ver?
*ah ZHAIN-chee POH-gee eer vayr?*

**Where do you live?**
Onde você mora?
*OWN-gee voe-SAY MOH-ra?*

**Earl, what city are you from?**
Earl, de que cidade você é?
*Earl, gee kee see-DAH-gee voe-SAY eh?*

**Is it a very large city?**
É uma cidade muito grande?
*eh OO-ma see-DAH-gee MOON-ee-too GRAN-gee?*

**Is there another available bathroom?**
Tem outro banheiro disponível?
*tayn OE-troo bahn-GNAY-roo gees-poe-NEE-vew?*

**How was your trip?**
Como foi a sua viagem?
*KOE-moo foy ah SOO-a vy-AH-zhayn?*

**Is the bathroom free?**
O banheiro está livre?
*oo bahn-GNAY-roo ees-TAH LEE-vree?*

**How are you feeling?**
Como você está se sentindo?
*KOE-moo voe-SAY ees-TAH see sain-TEEN-doo?*

**Do you have any recommendations?**
Você tem alguma recomendação?
*voe-SAY tayn ahw-GOOM-ah hay-kom-main-da-SAWM?*

**When did you first come to China?**
Quando você foi pra China pela primeira vez?
*KWAN-doo voe-SAY foy prah SHEE-na PAY-la pree-MAY-ra vays?*

**Were you born here?**
Você nasceu aqui?
*voe-SAY nah-SAY-oo ah-KEE?*

**Come join me for the rest of the vacation.**
Vem ficar comigo até o final das férias.
*vain fee-KAR ko-MEE-goo ah-TEH oo fy-NAW das FEH-ree-as.*

**What times do the shops open in this area?**
Que horas as lojas abrem nessa região?
*kee OH-ras ahs LOH-zhas AH-brain NEH-sa hay-zhee-AWM?*

**Is there tax-free shopping available?**
Tem loja de tax-free disponível?
*tayn LOH-zha gee tax-free gees-poe-NEE-vew?*

**Where can I change currency?**
Onde eu posso fazer o câmbio de moeda?
*OWN-gee AY-oo POH-soo fah-ZAYR oo KAM-byo gee moe-EH-da?*

**Is it legal to drink in this area?**
É permitido beber nesse lugar?
*eh payr-mee-CHEE-doo bay-BAYH NAY-sy loo-GAR?*

**Can I smoke in this area?**
Posso fumar nesse lugar?
*POH-soo foo-MAH NAY-sy loo-GAR?*

**What about this?**
E isso?
*ee EE-soo?*

**Can I park here?**
Posso estacionar aqui?
*POH-soo ees-tah-see-oe-NAH ah-KEE?*

**Have you gotten used to living in Spain by now?**
Você já se acostumou a morar na Espanha?
*voe-SAY zha see ah-koes-too-MOE ah moe-RAH nah ays-PAN-gna?*

**How much does it cost to park here?**
Quanto custa para estacionar aqui?
*KWAN-too KOOS-ta PAH-ra ees-ta-see-oe-NAH ah-KEE?*

**How long can I park here?**
Por quanto tempo eu posso deixar estacionado aqui?
Poor *KWAN-too TAYM-poo AY-oo POH-soo day-SHAR ays-ta-see-oe-nah-doo ah-KEE?*

**Where can I get some directions?**
Onde eu encontro as instruções?
*OWN-gee AY-oo ain-KON-troo ahs eens-troo-SON-ys?*

**Can you point me in the direction of the bridge?**
Você pode apontar pra onde é a ponte?
*voe-SAY POH-gee ah-pown-TAH prah OWN-gee eh ah POWN-chee?*

**What can I do here for fun?**
O que eu posso fazer aqui pra me divertir?
*oo kee AY-oo POH-soo fah-ZAYR ah-KEE prah mee gee-VAYH-cheer?*

**Is this a family-friendly place?**
Esse é um lugar amigável para família?
*AY-sy eh oom loo-GAR ah-mee-GAH-vew PAH-rah fam-MEE-lya?*

**Are kids allowed here?**
É permitido criança aqui?
*eh payr-mee-CHEE-doo kry-AN-sa ah-KEE?*

**Where can I find the park?**
Onde é o estacionamento?
*OWN-gee eh oo ees-TAH-see-oe-na-MAIN-too?*

**How do I get back to my hotel?**
Como eu volto pro hotel?
*KOE-moo AY-oo VOH-w-too proo oe-TEHW?*

**Where can I get some medicine?**
Onde eu acho remédio?
*OWN-gee AY-oo AH-shoo hay-MEH-gyo?*

**Is my passport safe here?**
O meu passaporte está seguro aqui?
*oo MAY-oo pa-sa-POHR-chee ees-TAH say-GOO-roo ah-KEE?*

**Do you have a safe for my passport and belongings?**
Você tem um cofre pro meu passaporte e pertences?
*voe-SAY tayn oom KOH-free proo MAY-oo pa-sa-POHR-chee y payh-TAYN-sees?*

**Is it safe to be here past midnight?**
É seguro ficar aqui depois da meia-noite?
*eh say-GOO-roo fee-KAR ah-KEE day-POYS da MAY-ah NOY-chee?*

**When is the best time to visit this shop?**
Qual é o melhor horário pra visitar essa loja?
*Kwaw eh oo may-LYOR oe-RAH-ryo prah vy-zy-TAH EH-sa LOH-zha?*

**What is the best hotel in the area?**
Qual é o melhor hotel na região?
*Kwaw eh oo may-LYOR oe-TEHW nah hay-zhee-AWM?*

**What attractions are close to my hotel?**
Quais atrações são próximas do meu hotel?
*KWA-ees ah-tra-SONN-ys sawm PROH-see-mas doo MAY-oo oe-TEHW?*

**Do you have any advice for tourists?**
Você tem algum conselho para turistas?
*voe-SAY tayn ahw-GOOM kon-SAY-lyo PAH-ra too-REES-tas?*

**Do you have a list of the top things to do in the area?**
Você tem uma lista das melhores coisas para fazer na região?
*voe-SAY tayn OO-ma LEES-ta das may-LYOH-rees KOY-zas prah fah-ZAYR nah hay-zhee-AWM?*

**What do I need to pack to go there?**
O que eu preciso levar pra lá?
*oo kee AY-oo pray-SEE-zoo lay-VAH prah lah?*

**Can you recommend me some good food to eat?**
Você pode me recomendar alguma comida boa para comer?
*voe-SAY POH-gee mee hay-koe-main-DAH ahw-GOOM-ah koe-MEE-da BOE-a PAH-ra koe-MEHR?*

**What should I do with my time here?**
Como eu poderia passar o tempo aqui?
*KOE-moo AY-oo poe-DAY-ree-a pah-SAR oo TAYM-poo ah-KEE?*

**What is the cheapest way to get from my hotel to the shop?**
Qual é a forma mais barata de ir do meu hotel pra loja?
*Kwaw eh ah FOHR-ma MAH-ees bah-RAH-ta gee eer doo MAY-oo oe-TEHW prah LOH-zha?*

**What do you think of my itinerary?**
O que você acha do meu itinerário?
*oo kee voe-SAY AH-sha doo MAY-oo ee-tee-nay-RAH-ryo?*

**Does my phone work in here in Brazil?**
O meu telefone funciona aqui no Brasil?
*oo MAY-oo tay-lay-FOE-nee foon-see-OE-na ah-KEE noo bra-ZYU?*

**What is the best route to get to my hotel?**
Qual é o melhor caminho pra ir para o meu hotel?
*Kwaw eh oo may-LYOR ka-MEEN-nyu PAH-ra eer PAHra oo MAY-oo oe-TEHW?*

**Will the weather be okay for outside activities?**
O clima vai estar bom para atividades ao ar livre?
*oo KLI-mah VAH-ee ees-TAH bown PAH-ra ah-chee-vee-DAH-gees AH-oo ah LEE-vree?*

**Was that rude?**
Foi uma grosseria?
*foy OO-ma groe-say-REE-a?*

**Where should I stay away from?**
Onde é que eu devo evitar ir?
*OWN-gee eh kee AY-oo DAY-voo ay-vee-TAH eeh?*

**What is the best dive site in the area?**
Qual é o melhor local para mergulho nesta região?
*kwaw eh oo may-LYOR loe-KAW PAH-ra mayh-GOO-lyu NEH-sa hay-zhee-AWM?*

**What is the best beach in the area?**
Qual é a melhor praia na região?
*Kwaw eh ah may-LYOR PRAH-ya nah hay-zhee-AWM?*

**Do I need reservations?**
Preciso fazer reserva?
*pray-SEE-zoo fah-ZAYR hay-ZEH-va?*

**I need directions to the best local food.**
Onde é o melhor lugar pra comer algo tradicional?
*OWN-gee eh oo may-LYOR loo-GAR PAH-ra koe-MEHR AHW-goo tra-gee-see-OE-naw?*

**What's your name?**
Qual é o seu nome?
*Kwaw eh oo SAY-oo NOE-me?*

**Where is the nearest place to eat?**
Qual é o lugar mais próximo para comer?
*Kwaw eh oo loo-GAR MAH-ees PROH-see-moo PAH-ra koe-MEHR?*

**Where is the nearest hotel?**
Qual é o hotel mais próximo?
*Kwaw eh oo oe-TEHW MAH-ees PROH-see-moo?*

**Where is transportation?**
Onde fica o transporte?
*OWN-gee FEE-ka oo trans-POH-chee?*

**How much is this?**
Quanto custa?
*KWAN-too KOOS-ta?*

**Do you pay tax here?**
Precisa pagar alguma taxa aqui?
*prAY-see-za pa-GAH ahw-GOOM-ah TAH-sha ah-KEE?*

**What types of payment are accepted?**
Vocês aceitam quais tipos de pagamento?
*voe-SAYS ah-SAY-tam KWA-ees CHEE-poos gee pah-gah-MAIN-too?*

**Can you help me read this?**
Você pode me ajudar a ler isso?
*voe-SAY POH-gee mee ah-zhoo-DAR ah layh EE-soo?*

**What languages do you speak?**
Quais são os idiomas que você fala?
*KWA-ees sawm oos ee-gee-OE-mas kee voe-SAY FAH-la?*

**Is it difficult to speak English?**
É difícil falar inglês?
*eh gy-FEE-seew fah-LAR een-GLAYS?*

**What does that mean?**
O que isso quer dizer?
*oo kee EE-soo kehr gee-ZAYR?*

**What is your name?**
Qual é o seu nome?
*Kwaw eh oo SAY-oo NOE-me?*

**Do you have a lighter?**
Você tem isqueiro?
*voe-SAY tayn ees-KAY-roo?*

**Do you have a match?**
Você tem fósforo?
*voe-SAY tayn FOHS-foe-roo?*

**Is this souvenir from your country?**
Esse souvenir é do seu país?
*AY-sy soo-vay-NEEH eh doo SAY-oo pah-EES?*

**What is this?**
O que é isso?
*oo kee eh EE-soo?*

**Can I ask you a question?**
Posso te fazer uma pergunta?
*POH-soo chee fah-ZAYR OO-ma payr-GOON-ta?*

**Where is the safest place to store my travel information?**
Qual é o lugar mais seguro para armazenar as informações de viagem?
*Kwaw eh oo loo-GAR MAH-ees say-GOO-roo PAH-ra ah-MAH-zee-nar ahs een-foeh-mah-SONN-ees gee vy-AH-zhayn?*

**Will you come along with me?**
Você vai comigo?
*voe-SAY VAH-ee ko-MEE-goo?*

**Is this your first time here?**
É a sua primeira vez aqui?
*eh ah SOO-a pree-MAY-ra vays ah-KEE?*

**What is your opinion on the matter?**
Qual é a sua opinião sobre isso?
*Kwaw eh ah SOO-a oe-pee-nee-AWM SOE-bree EE-soo?*

**Will this spoil if I leave it out too long?**
Vai estragar se eu deixar muito tempo fora da geladeira?
*VAH-ee ays-tra-GAH see AY-oo day-SHAR MOON-ee-too TAYM-poo FOH-ra da zhay-la-DAY-ra?*

**What side of the sidewalk do I walk on?**
Eu ando de que lado da calçada?
*AY-oo AN-doo gee kee LAH-doo dah kaw-SA-da?*

**What do those lights mean?**
O que significam essas luzes?
*oo kee seeg-nee-FEE-kam EH-sas LOO-zys?*

**Can I walk up these stairs?**
Posso subir essas escadas?
*POH-soo soo-BEEH EH-sas ay-KAH-das?*

**Is that illegal here?**
Isso é ilegal aqui?
*EE-soo eh ee-lay-GAW ah-KEE?*

**How much trouble would I get in if I did that?**
Seria muito ruim se eu fizesse isso?
*say-REE-ah MOON-ee-too hoo-EEN see AY-oo fee-ZEH-see EE-soo?*

**Why don't we all go together?**
Por que não vamos todos juntos?
*poor-KAY NANN-oo VAM-moos TOE-doos ZHOON-toos?*

**May I throw away waste here?**
Posso jogar o lixo aqui?
*POH-soo zhoe-GAR oo LEE-shoo ah-KEE?*

**Where is the recycle bin?**
Onde fica a lixeira de material reciclável?
*OWN-gee FEE-ka ah lee-SHAY-ra gee mah-tay-ree-AW hAY-sy-KLAH-vehw?*

# WHEN SOMEONE IS BEING RUDE

**Please, close your mouth while chewing that.**
Por favor, feche a boca quando estiver mastigando.
*Poer fa-VOER, FAY-shy ah BOE-ka KWAN-doo ays-chee-VEH mahs-chee-GAN-doo.*

**Don't ask me again, please.**
Não me pergunte de novo, por favor.
*NANN-oo mee payh-GOON-chee gee NOE-voo, poer fa-VOER.*

**I'm not paying for that.**
Não vou pagar isso.
*NANN-oo voe pa-GAH EE-soo.*

**Leave me alone or I am calling the authorities.**
Me deixe em paz ou eu vou chamar a polícia.
*Mee DAY-shee ayn PAH-ys oe AY-oo voe sha-MAH ah poe-LEE-cya.*

**Hurry up!**
Rápido!
*HAH-pee-doo!*

**Stop bothering me!**
Pare de me incomodar!
*PAH-ree gee mee een-koe-moe-DAH!*

**Don't bother me, please!**
Não me incomode, por favor!
*NANN-oo mee een-koe-MOE-gee poer fa-VOER!*

**Are you content?**
Você está feliz?
*voe-SAY ees-TAH fay-LEES?*

**I'm walking away, please don't follow me.**
Vou embora, por favor não me acompanhe.
*Voe ain-BOH-ra, poer fa-VOER NANN-oo mee ah-kom-PANN-gnee.*

**You stole my shoes and I would like them back.**
Você roubou os meus sapatos e eu preciso pegar eles de volta.
*voe-SAY hoe-BOE oos MEH-oos sah-PAH-toos y AY-oo pray-SEE-zoo pay-GAH AY-lys gee VOH-oo-ta.*

**You have the wrong person.**
Você tá mexendo com a pessoa errada.
*voe-SAY tah may-SHAIN-doo kom ah pay-SOE-ah ay-HA-dah.*

**I think you are incorrect.**
Acho que você está errado. (masc.) | Acho que você está errada. (fem.)
*AH-shoo kee voe-SAY ees-TAH ay-HA-doo (masc.) | AH-shoo kee voe-SAY ees-TAH ay-HA-dah (fem.)*

**Stop waking me up!**
Pare de me acordar!
*PAH-ree gee mee ah-koeh-DAH!*

**You're talking too much.**
Você está falando demais.
*voe-SAY ees-TAH fah-LAN-doo gee-MAH-ees.*

**That hurts!**
Tá doendo!
*tah doe-AIN-doo!*

**I need you to apologize.**
Preciso que você peça desculpas.
*pray-SEE-zoo kee voe-SAY PEH-sa gees-KOO-pas.*

**Stay away from my children!**
Fique longe dos meus filhos!
*FEE-ky LON-gee doos MAY-oos FEE-lyos!*

**Don't touch me.**
Não me toque.
*NANN-oo mee TOH-kee.*

**I would appreciate it if you didn't take my seat.**
Agradeço se você não pegar o meu lugar.
*Ah-grah-DAY-soo see voe-SAY NANN-oo pay-GAH oo MAY-oo loo-GAR.*

**You didn't tell me that.**
Você não me disse isso.
*voe-SAY NANN-oo mee GEE-see EE-soo.*

**You are price gouging me.**
Você está me cobrando o preço errado.
*voe-SAY ees-TAH mee koe-BRAN-doo oo PRAY-soo ay-HA-doo.*

**Please be quiet, I am trying to listen.**
Por favor, fique quieto, estou tentando escutar.
*poer fa-VOER, FEE-ky kee-EH-too, ees-TOE tayn-TAN-doo ays-koo-TAH.*

**Don't interrupt me while I am talking.**
Não me interrompa quando eu estiver falando.
*NANN-oo mee een-tay-HOEM-pah KWAN-doo AY-oo ays-chee-VEH fah-LAN-doo.*

**Don't sit on my car and stay away from it.**
Não sente no meu carro e fique longe dele.
*NANN-oo SAYN-chee noo MAY-oo KAH-hoo y FEE-ky LON-gee DAY-ly.*

**Get out of my car.**
Saia do meu carro.
*SAH-ya doo MAY-oo KAH-hoo.*

**Get away from me and leave me alone!**
Fique longe de mim e me deixe em paz!
*FEE-ky LON-gee meen y mee DAY-shee ayn PAH-ys!*

**You're being rude.**
Você está sendo mal-educado.
*Voe-SAY ees-TAH SAYN-doo MAH-oo ay-doo-KAH-doo.*

**Please don't curse around my children.**
Por favor, não xingue perto dos meus filhos.
*poer fa-VOER, NANN-oo SHEEN-guh PEAR-too dos MAY-oos FEE-lyos.*

**Let go of me!**
Me deixa!
*mee DAY-sha!*

**I'm not going to tell you again.**
Não vou te falar isso de novo.
*NANN-oo voe fah-LAR EE-soo gee NOE-voo.*

**Don't yell at me.**

Não grite comigo.

*NANN-oo GREE-chee ko-MEE-goo.*

**Please lower your voice.**

Por favor, abaixe a voz.

*poer fa-VOER, ah-BYE-shee ah VOH-ys.*

**What is the problem?**

Qual é o problema?

*Kwaw eh oo proe-BLAY-mah?*

**I would appreciate if you didn't take pictures of me.**

Por gentileza, não tire fotos de mim.

*Poeh zhain-chee-LAY-za, NANN-oo CHEE-ree FOH-toos gee meen.*

**I am very disappointed in the way you are behaving.**

Estou muito decepcionado com a forma que você está se comportando.

*ees-TOE MOON-ee-too day-sayp-syo-NAH-doo kom ah FOH-ma kee voe-SAY ees-TAH see kom-poe-TAN-doo.*

**Watch where you are walking!**

Tenha cuidado com onde você está andando!

*TAYN-gna kooy-DAH-doo kom OWN-gee voe-SAY ees-TAH ann-DANN-doo!*

**He just bumped into me!**

Ele acabou de esbarrar em mim!

*AY-ly ah-ka-BOE gee ays-ba-HAH ayn meen!*

# MEDICAL

**I would like to set up an appointment with my doctor.**
Gostaria de marcar uma consulta com o meu médico.
*goes-ta-REE-a gee mar-KAR OO-ma kon-SOO-ta kom oo MAY-oo MEH-gee-koo.*

**I am a new patient and need to fill out forms.**
Sou um paciente novo e preciso preencher o cadastro.
*Soe oom pah-see-AIN-chee NOE-voo y pray-SEE-zoo pray-AIN-shayh oo kah-DAHS-troo.*

**I am allergic to certain medications.**
Tenho alergia a alguns remédios.
*TAYN-gnoo ah-layh-GEE-ahh ah ahw-GOON-s hay-MEH-gyos.*

**That is where it hurts.**
É aí que tá doendo.
*Eh ah-EE kee tah doe-AIN-doo.*

**I have had the flu for three weeks.**
Estou gripado há três semanas.
*ees-TOE gree-PAH-doo ah trays say-MANN-nas.*

**It hurts when I walk on that foot.**
Esse pé dói quando eu ando.
*AY-sy peh DOH-y KWAN-doo AY-oo AN-doo.*

**When is my next appointment?**
Quando é a minha próxima consulta?
*KWAN-doo eh ah MEE-nya PROH-see-ma kon-SOO-tah?*

**Does my insurance cover this?**
O meu seguro cobre isso?
*oo MAY-oo say-GOO-roo KOH-bree EE-soo?*

**Do you want to take a look at my throat?**
Quer dar uma olhada na minha garganta?
*kehr dah OO-ma oe-LYA-da nah MEE-nya gar-GANN-ta?*

**Do I need to fast before going there?**
Preciso ficar em jejum antes de ir lá?
*pray-SEE-zoo fee-KAR ayn zhay-ZHOOM AHN-chees gee eer lah?*

**Is there a generic version of this medicine?**
Tem algum genérico desse remédio?
*tayn ahw-GOOM zhay-NEH-ree-koo DAY-sy hay-MEH-gyo?*

**I need to get back on dialysis.**
Preciso voltar a fazer diálise.
*pray-SEE-zoo voe-TAH ah fah-ZAYR GEE-ahH-lee-zee.*

**My blood type is A.**
O meu sangue é tipo A.
*oo MAY-oo SANN-ghee eh CHEE-poo ah.*

**I will be more than happy to donate blood.**
Vou ficar muito feliz em doar sangue.
*Voe fee-KAR MOON-ee-too fay-LEES ayn doe-AH SANN-ghee.*

**I have been feeling dizzy.**
Estou tonto.
*ees-TOE TON-too.*

**The condition is getting worse.**
Está piorando.
*ees-TAH pee-o-RAN-doo.*

**The medicine has made the condition a little better, but it is still there.**
O remédio está melhorando o problema, mas ele continua.
*Oo hay-MEH-gyo ays-TAH may-lyo-RAN-doo oo proe-BLAY-mah,MAH-ees AY-ly kon-chee-NOO-a.*

**Is my initial health examination tomorrow?**
O meu exame inicial é amanhã?
*oo MAY-oo ay-ZAM-mee ee-nee-see-AW eh ah-man-GNAN?*

**I would like to switch doctors.**
Eu gostaria de mudar de médico.
*AY-oo goes-ta-REE-a gee moo-DAR gee MEH-gee-koo.*

**Can you check my blood pressure?**
Você pode verificar a minha pressão?
*voe-SAY POH-gee vay-ree-fee-KAR ah MEE-nya pray-SAWM?*

**I have a fever that won't go away.**
Estou com uma febre persistente.
*ees-TOE kom OO-ma FEH-bree payr-sees-TAYN-tee.*

**I think my arm is broken.**
Acho que o meu braço está quebrado.
*AH-shoo kee oo MAY-oo BRAH-soo ees-TAH kay-BRAH-doo.*

**I think I have a concussion.**
Acho que levei uma pancada.
*AH-shoo kee lay-VAY OO-ma pann-KAH-da.*

**My eyes refuse to focus.**
Os meus olhos não estão focando.
*oos MAY-oos OH-lyos NANN-oo ees-TAWM foe-KAN-doo.*

**I have double vision.**
Estou vendo tudo duplicado.
*ees-TOE VAIN-doo TOO-doo doo-plee-KAH-doo.*

**Is surgery the only way to fix this?**
O único jeito de melhorar é com cirurgia?
*oo OO-ny-koo ZHAY-to gee may-lyo-RAR eh kom see-rooh-ZHEE-a?*

**Who are you referring me to?**
Para quem você está me encaminhando?
*PAH-ra kayn voe-SAY ees-TAH mee ain-ka-meen-GNAN-doo?*

**Where is the waiting room?**
Onde é a sala de espera?
*OWN-gee eh ah SAH-la gee ees-PEH-ra?*

**Can I bring someone with me into the office?**
Posso levar alguém comigo para o consultório?
*POH-soo lay-VAH AHW-gain ko-MEE-goo PAH-ra oo kon-soo-TOH-ryo?*

**I need help filling out these forms.**
Preciso de ajuda para preencher esse cadastro.
*pray-SEE-zoo gee ah-ZHOO-da PAH-ra pray-ain-SHAYH AY-sy ka-DAHS-troo.*

**Do you take Cobra as an insurance provider?**
Vocês aceitam Cobra como seguro de saúde?
*voe-SAYS ah-SAY-tam KOH-bra KOE-moo say-GOO-roo gee sah-OO-gee?*

**What is my copayment?**
Qual é o meu copagamento?
*kwaw eh oo MAY-oo koe-pah-gah-MAIN-to?*

**What forms of payment do you accept?**
Que tipos de pagamento vocês aceitam?
*Kee CHEE-poos gee pah-gah-MAIN-to voe-SAYS ah-SAY-tam?*

**Do you have a payment plan, or is it all due now?**
Posso parcelar ou tenho que pagar tudo agora?
*POH-soo pah-say-LAH TOO-doo oe TAYN-gnoo kee pa-GAH TOO-doo ah-GOH-ra?*

**My old doctor prescribed something different.**
O meu antigo médico me prescreveu outra coisa.
*oo MAY-oo an-CHEE-goo MEH-gee-koo mme prays-kray-VAY-yu OE-tra KOY-za.*

**Will you take a look at my leg?**
Você dá uma olhada na minha perna?
*voe-SAY dah OO-ma oe-LYAH-da nah MEE-nya PEH-na?*

**I need to be referred to a gynecologist.**
Preciso ser transferida para um ginecologista.
*pray-SEE-zoo sayh trans-fay-REE-da PAH-ra oom zhee-nay-koe-loe-ZHEES-ta.*

**I am unhappy with the medicine you prescribed me.**
Não estou satisfeito com o remédio que você me prescreveu.
*NANN-oo ees-TOE sah-chees-FAY-to kom oo hay-MEH-gyo kee voe-SAY mee prays-kray-VAY-yu.*

**Do you see patients on the weekend?**
Você atende no final de semana?
*Voe-SAY ah-TAYN-gee noo fy-NAW gee say-MANN-na?*

**I need a good therapist.**
Preciso de um bom terapeuta.
*pray-SEE-zoo gee oom bown tay-rah-PAY-oo-ta.*

**How long will it take me to rehab this injury?**
Quanto tempo vai demorar para eu me recuperar dessa lesão?
*KWAN-too TAYM-poo VAH-ee day-moe-RAH PAH-ra AY-oo mee hay-koo-PAY-rah DEH-sa lay-ZAWM?*

**I have not gone to the bathroom in over a week.**
Não vou ao banheiro há mais de uma semana.
*NANN-oo voe MAH-ees AH-oo bahn-GNAY-roo ah MAH-ees gee OO-ma say-MANN-na.*

**I am constipated and feel bloated.**
Estou com constipação e me sentindo inchado.
*ees-TOE kom kons-chee-pah-SAWM y mee sain-TEEN-doo een-SHAH-doo.*

**It hurts when I go to the bathroom.**
Dói quando eu vou ao banheiro.
*DOH-y KWAN-doo AY-oo voe AH-oo bahn-GNAY-roo.*

**I have not slept well at all since getting here.**
Não consegui dormir bem desde que cheguei aqui.
*NANN-oo kon-say-GHEE doeh-MEEH bayn shay-GAY ah-KEE.*

**Do you have any pain killers?**
Você tem algum analgésico?
*voe-SAY tayn ahw-GOOM ah-now-ZHEH-zee-koo?*

**I am allergic to that medicine.**
Tenho alergia a esse remédio.
*TAYN-gnoo ah-layr-GEE-ahh AY-sy hay-MEH-gyo.*

**How long will I be under observation?**
Por quanto tempo eu vou ficar em observação?
*Poeh KWAN-too TAYM-poo AY-oo voe fee-KAR ayn oe-bee-say-vah-SAWM?*

**I have a toothache.**
Estou com dor de dente.
*ees-TOE kom doeh gee DAYN-chee.*

**Do I need to see a dentist?**
Preciso ir a um dentista?
*pray-SEE-zoo eer ah oom dayn-CHEES-ta?*

**Does my insurance cover dental?**
O meu seguro de saúde cobre dentista?
*Oo MAY-oo say-GOO-roo gee sah-OO-gee KOH-bree dayn-CHEES-ta?*

**My diarrhea won't go away.**
Continuo com diarreia.
*kon-chee-NOO kom GEE-ahh-HEH-ya.*

**Can I have a copy of the receipt for my insurance?**
Posso ficar com uma cópia do recibo, para mostrar ao seguro?
*POH-soo fee-KAR kom OO-ma KOH-pya doo hay-SEE-boo, PAH-ra moes-TRAH AH-oo say-GOO-roo?*

**I need a pregnancy test.**
Preciso fazer um teste de gravidez.
*pray-SEE-zoo fah-ZAYR oom TEHS-chee gee grah-vee-DAYS.*

**I think I may be pregnant.**
Acho que posso estar grávida.
*AH-shoo kee POH-soo ays-TAH GRAH-vy-da.*

**Can we please see a pediatrician?**
Podemos ir a um pediatra?
*po-DAY-moos eer ah oom pay-GEE-ahH-tra?*

**I have had trouble breathing.**
Estou com dificuldade de respirar.
*ees-TOE kom gee-fee-koo-DAH-gee gee hays-PEE-rah.*

**My sinuses are acting up.**
A minha sinusite está atacada.
*ah MEE-nya sy-noo-ZEE-chy ees-TAH ah-ta-KA-da.*

**Will I still be able to breastfeed?**
Ainda vou poder amamentar?
*ah-EEN-da voe poe-DAYH ah-ma-main-TAH?*

**How long do I have to stay in bed?**
Por quanto tempo vou precisar ficar de cama?
*pooh KWAN-too TAYM-poo voe pray-see-ZAR fee-KAR gee KAM-ma?*

**How long do I have to stay under hospital care?**
Por quanto tempo vou ter que ficar no hospital?
*pooh KWAN-too TAYM-poo voe tayh kee fee-KAR noo oes-py-TAH-oo?*

**Is it contagious?**
É contagioso?
*eh kon-ta-gy-OE-zoo?*

**How far along am I?**
Estou melhorando?
*Ees-TOE may-lyor-AN-doo?*

**What did the x-ray say?**
O que o Raio-X está dizendo?
*oo kee oo HYE-oo shees ees-TAH gee-ZAIN-doo?*

**Can I walk without a cane?**
Vou poder andar sem bengala?
*voe poe-DAYH an-DAH sayn bayn-GA-la?*

**Is the wheelchair necessary?**
Vou precisar de cadeira de rodas?
*Voe pray-see-ZAR gee ka-DAY-ra gee HOH-das?*

**Am I in the right area of the hospital?**
Estou no setor certo do hospital?
*ees-TOE noo say-TOEH SEH-too doo oes-py-TAH-oo?*

**Where is the front desk receptionist?**
Onde fica a recepção?
*OWN-gee FEE-ka ah hay-say-pee-SAWM?*

**I would like to go to a different waiting area.**
Eu gostaria de ir para outra sala de espera.
*AY-oo goes-ta-REE-a gee eer PAH-ra OE-tra SAH-la gee ees-PEH-ra.*

**Can I have a change of sheets, please?**
Podem trocar os meus lençóis, por favor?
*POH-dayn troe-KAH MAY-oos MAY-oos layn-SOYS, poer fa-VOER?*

**Excuse me, what is your name?**
Desculpa, qual é o seu nome?
*gees-KOO-pa, kwaw eh oo SAY-oo NOE-me?*

**Who is the doctor in charge here?**
Quem é o médico responsável?
*kayn eh oo MEH-gee-koo hays-pon-SAH-vew?*

**I need some assistance, please.**
Estou precisando de ajuda.
*ees-TOE prAY-sy-ZAN-doo gee ah-ZHOO-da.*

### Will my recovery affect my ability to do work?
A minha recuperação vai afetar a minha capacidade para trabalhar?
*ah MEE-nya hay-koo-pay-ra-SAWM VAH-ee ah-fay-TAH ah MEE-nya ka-pa-see-DAH-gee PAH-ra tra-ba-LYAR?*

### How long is the estimated recovery time?
Qual é o tempo previsto para recuperação?
*kwaw eh oo TAYM-poo pray-VEES-too PAH-ra hay-koo-pay-ra-SAWM?*

### Is that all you can do for me? There has to be another option.
Isso é tudo que você pode fazer por mim? Tem que ter alguma outra opção.
*EE-soo eh TOO-doo kee voe-SAY POH-gee fah-ZAYR poeh meen? tayn kee tayh ahw-GOOM-ah OE-tra oep-SAWM.*

### I need help with motion sickness.
Preciso de ajuda, estou com enjoo.
*pray-SEE-zoo gee ah-ZHOO-da, ees-TOE kom ayn-ZHOE.*

### I'm afraid of needles.
Tenho medo de agulha.
*TAYN-gnoo MAY-doo gee ah-GOO-lya.*

### My gown is too small; I need another one.
Minha roupa é muito pequena; preciso de outra.
*MEE-nya HOE-pa eh MOON-ee-too pay-KEN-na; pray-SEE-zoo gee OE-tra.*

### Can I have extra pillows?
Posso pedir outros travesseiros?
*POH-soo pay-GEEH OE-troos trah-vy-SAY-roos?*

### I need assistance getting to the bathroom.
Preciso de ajuda para ir ao banheiro.
*pray-SEE-zoo gee ah-ZHOO-da PAH-ra eer AH-oo bahn-GNAY-roo.*

### Hi, is the doctor in?
Oi, o doutor está?
*OE-y, oo doe-TOEH ees-TAH?*

### When should I schedule the next checkup?
Para quando devo agendar o próximo exame?
*PAH-ra KWAN-doo DAY-voo ah-zhayn-DAH oo PROH-see-moo ay-ZAM-mee?*

**When can I have these stitches removed?**
Quando vou poder tirar os pontos?
*KWAN-doo voe poe-DAYH chee-RAH oos PON-toos?*

**Do you have any special instructions while I'm in this condition?**
Você tem alguma recomendação especial para essa minha condição?
*voe-SAY tayn ahw-GOOM-ah hay-kom-main-da-SAWM ays-pay-see-AH-oo PAH-ra EH-sa MEE-nya kon-gee-SAWM?*

# ORDERING FOOD

**Can I see the menu?**
Posso ver o cardápio?
*POH-soo vayh oo kah-DAH-pyo?*

**I'm really hungry. We should eat something soon.**
Estou com muita fome. A gente precisa comer logo.
*ees-TOE kom MOON-ee-ta FOE-my. ah ZHAIN-chee prAY-sy-za koe-MEHR LOH-goo.*

**Can I take a look in the kitchen?**
Posso dar uma olhada na cozinha?
*POH-soo dah OO-ma oe-LYA-da nah koe-ZEEN-nya?*

**Can we see the drink menu?**
Podemos ver o cardápio de bebidas?
*po-DAY-moos vayh oo kah-DAH-pyo gee bay-BEE-das?*

**When can we be seated?**
Quando a gente vai poder sentar?
*KWAN-doo ah ZHAIN-chee VAH-ee poe-DAYH sayn-TAH?*

**This is very tender and delicious.**
Está muito macio e gostoso.
*ees-TAH MOON-ee-too mah-SEE-oo y goes-TOE-zoo.*

**Do you serve alcohol?**
Vocês servem bebidas alcoólicas?
*voe-SAYS SEH-vayn bay-BEE-das ahw-KOH-ly-kas?*

**I'm afraid our party can't make it.**
Acho que o nosso grupo não vai conseguir chegar.
*AH-shoo kee oo NOH-soo GROO-poo NANN-oo VAH-ee kon-say-GHEEH shay-GAH.*

**That room is reserved for us.**
Esse salão está reservado para nós.
*AY-see sah-LAWM ees-TAH hay-zur-VAH-doo PAH-ra NOH-ys.*

### Are there any seasonal favorites that you serve?
Vocês estão servindo algum prato favorito da estação?
*voe-SAYS ees-TAWM sayr-VEEN-doo ahw-GOOM PRAH-too fah-voe-REE-too dah ees-tah-SAWM?*

### Do you offer discounts for kids or seniors?
Vocês dão desconto para crianças ou idosos?
*voe-SAYS dawm days-KON-too PAH-ra kry-AN-sas oe ee-DOH-zoos?*

### I would like it filleted.
Eu gostaria que fosse cortado em filés.
*AY-oo goes-ta-REE-a kee FOE-sy koeh-TAH-doo ayn fee-LEHS.*

### I would like to reserve a table for a party of four.
Gostaria de reservar uma mesa para um grupo de quatro pessoas.
*goes-ta-REE-a gee hay-zayh-VAH OO-ma MAY-za PAH-ra oom GROO-poo gee KWA-tro pay-SOE-ahs.*

### I would like to place the reservation under my name.
Gostaria de fazer uma reserva no meu nome.
*goes-ta-REE-a gee fah-ZAYR OO-ma hay-ZEH-va noo MAY-oo NOE-me.*

### What type of alcohol do you serve?
Que tipos de bebidas alcoólicas vocês têm?
*Kee CHEE-poos gee bay-BEE-das ahw-KOH-ly-kas voe-SAYS tayn?*

### Do I need a reservation?
Preciso fazer reserva?
*pray-SEE-zoo fah-ZAYR hay-ZEH-va?*

### What does it come with?
Quais são os acompanhamentos?
*KWA-ees sawm oos ah-kom-pann-gna-MAIN-toos?*

### What are the ingredients?
Quais são os ingredientes?
*KWA-ees sawm oos een-gray-GEE-ahYN-chees?*

### What else does the chef put in the dish?
O que mais o chefe coloca no prato?
*oo kay MAH-ees oo SHEH-fee koe-LOH-ka noo PRAH-too?*

**I wonder which of these tastes better?**
Qual dos dois você recomenda?
*kwaw doos doys voe-SAY hay-kom-MAIN-da?*

**That is incorrect. Our reservation was at noon.**
Está errado. A nossa reserva foi para o meio-dia.
*ees-TAH ay-HA-doo. ah NOH-sa hay-ZEH-va foy PAH-ra oo MAY-oo GEE-ahh.*

**I would like red wine, please.**
Eu gostaria de um vinho tinto, por favor.
*AY-oo goes-ta-REE-a gee oom VEEN-gnoo CHEEN-too, poer fa-VOER.*

**Can you choose the soup?**
Pode escolher a sopa?
*POH-gee ays-koe-LYEH ah SOE-pa?*

**What is the most popular dish here?**
Qual é o prato mais pedido aqui?
*kwaw eh oo PRAH-too MAH-ees pay-GEE-doo ah-KEE?*

**What are the specials today?**
Quais são os pratos do dia?
*KWA-ees sawm oos PRAH-toos doo GEE-ahh?*

**What are your appetizers?**
O que tem para aperitivo?
*oo kee tayn PAH-ra ah-pay-ree-CHEE-voo?*

**Please bring these out separately.**
Por favor, traga em pratos separados.
*poer fa-VOER, TRA-ga ayn PRAH-toos say-pa-RAH-doos.*

**Do we leave a tip?**
Vamos dar gorjeta?
*VAM-moos dah goeh-ZHAY-ta?*

**Are tips included with the bill?**
A conta inclui a gorjeta?
*Ah KON-ta een-KLOOY ah goeh-ZHAY-ta?*

**Split the bill, please.**
Faça contas separadas, por favor.
*FAH-sa KON-tas say-pa-RAH-das, poer fa-VOER.*

**We are paying separately.**
Estamos pagando separadamente.
*ees-TAM-moos pah-GAN-doo say-pa-ra-da-MAYN-chee.*

**Is there an extra fee for sharing an entrée?**
Precisamos pagar a mais se dividirmos o prato de entrada?
*pray-see-ZAM-moos pa-GAH MAH-ees see gee-vee-GEER-moos oo PRAH-too gee ayn-TRA-da?*

**Is there a local specialty that you recommend?**
Você pode recomendar algum prato regional?
*voe-SAY POH-gee hay-koe-main-DAH ahw-GOOM PRAH-too hay-gee-oe-NANN-oo?*

**This looks different from what I originally ordered.**
Acho que não foi isso que eu pedi.
*AH-shoo kee NANN-oo foy EE-soo kee AY-oo pay-GEE.*

**Is this a self-serve buffet?**
É um buffet self-service?
*eh oom bee-FAY self-service?*

**I want a different waiter.**
Quero outro garçom.
*KEH-roo OE-troo gah-SOEM.*

**Please move us to a different table.**
Você pode colocar a gente em outra mesa?
*voe-SAY POH-gee koe-loe-KAH ah ZHAIN-chee ayn OE-tra MAY-za?*

**Can we put two tables together?**
Podemos juntar duas mesas?
*po-DAY-moos joon-TAR DOO-as MAY-zas?*

**My spoon is dirty. Can I have another one?**
A minha colher está suja. Você pode trazer outra?
*ah MEE-nya koe-LYEH ees-TAH SOO-zha. voe-SAY POH-gee trah-ZAYH OE-tra?*

**We need more napkins, please.**
Precisamos de mais guardanapos, por favor.
*pray-see-ZAM-moos gee MAH-ees guah-da-NAH-poos, poer fa-VOER.*

**I'm a vegetarian and don't eat meat.**
Male: Sou vegetariano e não como carne.
*soe vay-zhay-ta-ree-AN-noo y NANN-oo KOE-moo KAH-nee.*
Female: Sou vegetariana e não como carne.
*soe vay-zhay-ta-ree-AN-na y NANN-oo KOE-moo KAH-nee.*

**The table next to us is being too loud. Can you say something?**
A mesa ao nosso lado está muito barulhenta. Você pode conversar com eles, por favor?
*ah MAY-za AH-oo NOH-soo LAH-doo ees-TAH MOON-ee-too bah-roo-LYEN-ta. voe-SAY POH-gee kon-vayh-SAH kom poer fa-VOER?*

**Someone is smoking in our non-smoking section.**
Alguém está fumando no nosso espaço de não-fumantes.
*AHW-gain ees-TAH foo-MAN-doo noo NOH-soo ees-PAH-soo gee NANN-oo foo-MAHN-chees.*

**Please seat us in a booth.**
Em qual mesa podemos sentar?
*ayn kwaw MAY-za po-DAY-moos sayn-TAH?*

**Do you have any non-alcoholic beverages?**
Vocês têm bebidas sem álcool?
*voe-SAYS tayn bay-BEE-das sayn AHW-koe?*

**Where is your bathroom?**
Onde é o banheiro?
*OWN-gee eh oo bahn-GNAY-roo?*

**Are you ready to order?**
Estão prontos para fazer o pedido?
*ees-TAWM PRON-toos PAH-ra fah-ZAYR oo pay-GEE-doo?*

**Five more minutes, please.**
Mais cinco minutos, por favor.
*MAH-ees SEEN-ko my-NOO-toos, poer fa-VOER.*

**What time do you close?**
Vocês fecham a que horas?
*voe-SAYS FAY-sham ah kee OH-ras?*

**Is there pork in this dish? I don't eat pork.**
Tem carne de porco nesse prato? Eu não como carne de porco.

*tayn KAH-nee gee POER-koo NAY-sy PRAH-too? AY-oo NANN-oo KOE-moo KAH-nee gee POER-koo.*

**Do you have any dishes for vegans?**

Vocês têm algum prato para veganos?

*voe-SAYS tayn ahw-GOOM PRAH-too PAH-ra vay-G ANN-noos?*

**Are these vegetables fresh?**

Esses legumes são de hoje?

*AY-sys lay-GOOM-mees sawm gee OE-zhee?*

**Has any of these vegetables been cooked in butter?**

Algum desses legumes foram cozidos na manteiga?

*ahw-GOOM DAY-sys lay-GOOM-mees foh-RAM koe-ZEE-doos nah man-TAY-ga?*

**Is this spicy?**

É picante?

*eh pee-KAN-chee?*

**Is this sweet?**

É doce?

*eh DOE-see?*

**I want more, please.**

Quero mais, por favor.

*KEH-roo MAH-ees, poer fa-VOER.*

**I would like a dish containing these items.**

Eu gostaria de um prato com esses itens.

*AY-oo goes-ta-REE-a gee oom PRAH-too kom AY-sys EE-tayns.*

**Can you make this dish light? Thank you.**

Vocês podem fazer esse prato numa versão light? Obrigado.

*voe-SAYS POH-dayn fah-ZAYR AY-sy PRAH-too NOO-ma vayh-SAWM light? oe-bree-GAH-doo.*

**Nothing else.**

Mais nada.

*MAH-ees NAH-da.*

**Please clear the plates.**

Você pode limpar os pratos, por favor?

*voe-SAY POH-gee leem-PAH oos PRAH-toos, poer fa-VOER?*

**May I have a cup of soup?**
Uma sopa, por favor.
*OO-ma SOE-pa, poer fa-VOER.*

**Do you have any bar snacks?**
Vocês servem algum lanche?
*voe-SAYS SEH-vayn ahw-GOOM LAN-shee?*

**Another round, please.**
Mais uma rodada, por favor.
*MAH-ees OO-ma hoe-DA-da, poer fa-VOER.*

**When is closing time for the bar?**
Que horas o bar fecha?
*kee OH-ras oo bah FAY-sha?*

**That was delicious!**
Estava muito gostoso!
*ees-TAH-va MOON-ee-too goes-TOE-zoo!*

**Does this have alcohol in it?**
Tem álcool?
*tayn AHW-koe?*

**Does this have nuts in it?**
Tem nozes nisso?
*tayn NOH-zees NEE-soo?*

**Is this gluten free?**
É sem glúten?
*eh sayn GLOO-tayn?*

**Can I get this to go?**
Pode ser para viagem?
*POH-gee sayh PAH-ra vy-AH-zhayn?*

**May I have a refill?**
Posso fazer um refil?
*POH-soo fah-ZAYR oom hay-FEEW?*

**Is this dish kosher?**
Esse prato é kosher?
*AY-sy PRAH-too eh KOH-sher?*

**I would like to change my drink.**
Gostaria de trocar a minha bebida.
*goes-ta-REE-a gee troe-KAH ah MEE-nya bay-BEE-da.*

**My coffee is cold. Could you please warm it up?**
O meu café está frio. Você pode esquentar, por favor?
*oo MAY-oo ka-FEH ees-TAH FREE-oo. voe-SAY POH-gee ays-kayn-TAH poer fa-VOER?*

**Do you serve coffee?**
Vocês têm café?
*voe-SAYS tayn ka-FEH?*

**Can I please have cream in my coffee?**
O café pode ser com creme?
*oo ka-FEH POH-gee sayh kom KRAYM-mee?*

**Please add extra sugar to my coffee.**
Por favor, coloque mais açúcar no meu café.
*poer fa-VOER, koe-LOH-kee MAH-ees ah-SOO-kah noo MAY-oo ka-FEH.*

**I would like to have my coffee served black, no cream and no sugar.**
Quero meu café preto, sem leite nem açúcar.
*KEH-roo MAY-oo ka-FEH PRAY-too, sain LAY-chee nain ah-SOO-kah.*

**I would like to have decaffeinated coffee, please.**
Quero café descafeinado, por favor.
*KEH-roo ka-FEH days-ka-fay-NAH-doo, poer fa-VOER.*

**Do you serve coffee-flavored ice cream?**
Vocês têm sorvete de café?
*voe-SAYS tayn soeh-VAY-chee gee ka-FEH?*

**Please put my cream and sugar on the side so that I can add it myself.**
Por favor, traga o leite e o açúcar por fora, para que eu mesmo coloque.
*poer fa-VOER, TRA-ga oo LAY-chee y oo ah-SOO-kah poeh FOH-ra, PAH-ra kee AY-oo MAYZ-moo koe-LOH-kee.*

**I would like to order an iced coffee.**
Quero um café gelado, por favor.
*KEH-roo oom ka-FEH zhay-LAH-doo, poer fa-VOER.*

**I would like an espresso please.**
Quero um café expresso, por favor.
*KEH-roo oom ka-FEH, poer fa-VOER.*

**Do you have 2% milk?**
Vocês têm leite desnatado?
*voe-SAYS tayn LAY-chee days-na-TAH-doo?*

**Do you serve soy milk?**
Vocês têm leite de soja?
*voe-SAYS tayn LAY-chee gee SOH-zha?*

**Do you have almond milk?**
Vocês têm leite de amêndoa?
*voe-SAYS tayn LAY-chee gee ah-MAIN-doe-a?*

**Are there any alternatives to the milk you serve?**
Tem alguma outra opção, além do leite que vocês têm?
*tayn ahw-GOOM-ah OE-tra oep-SAWM, ah-LAYN doo LAY-chee kee voe-SAYS tayn?*

**Please put the lemons for my tea on the side.**
Por favor, traga à parte os limões para o meu chá.
*poer fa-VOER, TRA-ga ah PAH-chee oos lee-MONN-ees PAH-ra oo MAY-oo shah.*

**No lemons with my tea, thank you.**
Sem limão no meu chá, obrigado.
*sayn lee-MANN-oo noo MAY-oo shah, oe-bree-GAH-doo.*

**Is your water from the tap?**
A água é da torneira?
*ah AH-gwa eh dah toeh-NAY-ra?*

**Sparkling water, please.**
Água com gás, por favor.
*AH-gwa kom GAH-ees, poer fa-VOER.*

**Can I get a diet coke?**
Uma coca diet, por favor.
*OO-ma KOH-ka diet, poer fa-VOER.*

**We're ready to order.**
Estamos prontos para pedir.
*ees-TAM-moos PRON-toos PAH-ra pay-GEEH.*

**Can we be seated over there instead?**
Em vez daqui, podemos sentar ali?
*ayn vays dah-KEE, po-DAY-moos sayn-TAH ah-LEE?*

**Can we have a seat outside?**
Podemos sentar do lado de fora?
*po-DAY-moos sayn-TAH doo LAH-doo gee FOH-ra?*

**Please hold the salt.**
Pouco sal, por favor.
*POE-koo SAH-oo, poer fa-VOER.*

**This is what I would like for my main course.**
Queremos isso como prato principal.
*kay-RAY-moos EE-soo KOE-moo PRAH-too pryn-see-PAHW.*

**I would like the soup instead of the salad.**
Gostaria dessa sopa no lugar da salada.
*goes-ta-REE-a DEH-sa SOE-pa noo loo-GAR dah sah-LAH-da.*

**I'll have the chicken risotto.**
Quero o risotto de frango.
*KEH-roo oo hee-ZOE-to gee FRAN-goo.*

**Can I change my order?**
Posso mudar o meu pedido?
*POH-soo moo-DAR oo MAY-oo pay-GEE-doo?*

**Do you have a kids' menu?**
Vocês têm um cardápio para crianças?
*voe-SAYS tayn oom kah-DAH-pyo PAH-ra kry-AN-sas?*

**When does the lunch menu end?**
Até que horas podemos pedir almoço?
*ah-TEH kee OH-ras po-DAY-moos pay-GEEH ahw-MOE-soo?*

**When does the dinner menu start?**
Que horas começa o jantar?
*kee OH-ras koe-MEH-sa oo zhan-TAH?*

**Do you have any recommendations from the menu?**
Você recomenda alguma coisa do cardápio?
*voe-SAY hay-kom-MAIN-da ahw-GOOM-ah KOY-za doo kah-DAH-pyo?*

**I would like to place an off-menu order.**
Gostaria de pedir algo que não está no cardápio.
*goes-ta-REE-a gee pay-GEEH AHW-goo kee NANN-oo ees-TAH noo kah-DAH-pyo.*

**Can we see the dessert menu?**
Podemos ver o cardápio de sobremesas?
*po-DAY-moos vayh oo kah-DAH-pyo gee soe-bray-MAY-zas?*

**Is this available sugar-free?**
Tem isso aqui sem açúcar?
*tayn EE-soo ah-KEE sayn ah-SOO-kah?*

**May we have the bill, please?**
A conta, por favor.
*ah KON-ta, poer fa-VOER.*

**Where do we pay?**
Onde pagamos?
*OWN-gee pa-GAM-moos?*

**Hi, we are with the party of Isaac.**
Oi, estamos na mesa do Isaac.
*OE-y, ees-TAM-moos nah MAY-za doo ee-ZAK.*

**We haven't made up our minds yet on what to order. Can we have a few more minutes, please?**
Ainda não decidimos o que pedir. Pode voltar em mais alguns minutos, por favor?
*ah-EEN-da NANN-oo day-see-GEE-moos oo kee pay-GEEH. POH-gee voe-TAH ayn MAH-ees ahw-GOON-s my-NOO-toos, poer fa-VOER?*

**Waiter!**
Garçom!
*gah-SOEM!*

**Waitress!**
Garçonete!
*gah-soe-NEH-chee!*

**I'm still deciding, come back to me, please.**
Ainda estou decidindo, volte depois, por favor.
*ah-EEN-da ees-TOE dAY-sy-DEEN-doo, VOH-oo-chee day-POYS, poer fa-VOER.*

**Can we have a pitcher of that?**
Podemos pedir uma jarra disso?
*po-DAY-moos pay-GEEH OO-ma ZHA-ha GEE-soo?*

**This is someone else's meal.**
Essa é a comida de outra pessoa.
*EH-sa eh ah koe-MEE-da gee OE-tra pay-SOE-ah.*

**Can you please heat this up a little more?**
Pode esquentar um pouco mais, por favor?
*POH-gee ays-kayn-TAH oom POE-koo MAH-ees, poer fa-VOER?*

**I'm afraid I didn't order this.**
Acho que não pedi isso.
*AH-shoo kee NANN-oo pay-GEE EE-soo.*

**The same thing again, please.**
A mesma coisa de novo, por favor.
*ah MAYZ-ma KOY-za gee NOE-voo, poer fa-VOER.*

**Can we have another bottle of wine?**
Você pode trazer outra garrafa de vinho?
*voe-SAY POH-gee trah-ZAYH OE-tra gah-HA-fa gee VEEN-gnoo?*

**That was perfect, thank you!**
Estava perfeito, obrigado!
*ees-TAH-va payh-FAY-too, oe-bree-GAH-doo!*

**Everything was good.**
Tudo estava gostoso.
*TOO-doo ees-TAH-va goes-TOE-zoo.*

**Can we have the bill?**
Pode trazer a conta?
*POH-gee trah-ZAYH ah KON-ta?*

**I'm sorry, but this bill is incorrect.**
Desculpe, mas essa conta está errada.
*gees-KOO-pee, MAH-ees EH-sa KON-ta ees-TAH ay-HA-dah.*

**Can I have clean cutlery?**
Você pode trazer talheres limpos?
*voe-SAY POH-gee trah-ZAYH tah-LYEH-rys LEEM-poos?*

**Can we have more napkins?**
Você pode trazer mais guardanapos?
*voe-SAY POH-gee trah-ZAYH MAH-ees guah-da-NAH-poos?*

**May I have another straw?**
Você pode trazer mais um canudo?
*voe-SAY POH-gee trah-ZAYH MAH-ees oom ka-NOO-doo?*

**What sides can I have with that?**
Quais acompanhamentos eu posso pedir?
*KWA-ees ah-kom-pann-gna-MAIN-toos AY-oo POH-soo pay-GEEH?*

**Excuse me, but this is overcooked.**
Desculpa, mas passou do ponto.
*gees-KOO-pa, MAH-ees pah-SOE doo PON-too.*

**May I talk to the chef?**
Posso falar com o cozinheiro?
*POH-soo fah-LAR kom oo koe-zee-GNAY-roo?*

**We have booked a table for fifteen people.**
Reservamos uma mesa para quinze pessoas.
*hay-zay-VAM-moos 00-ma MAY-za PAH-ra KEEN-zee pay-SOE-ahs.*

**Are there any tables free?**
Tem alguma mesa livre?
*tayn ahw-GOOM-ah MAY-za LEE-vree?*

**I would like one beer, please.**
Uma cerveja, por favor.
*OO-ma sayh-VAY-zha, poer fa-VOER.*

**Can you add ice to this?**
Você pode colocar gelo aqui?
*voe-SAY POH-gee koe-loe-KAH ZHAY-loo ah-KEE?*

**I would like to order a dark beer.**
Quero uma cerveja escura.
*KEH-roo OO-ma sayh-VAY-zha.*

**Do you have any beer from the tap?**
Tem chope?
*tayn SHOW-pee?*

**How expensive is your champagne?**
Quanto custa o champanhe de vocês?
*KWAN-too KOOS-ta oo sham-PAN-gnee gee voe-SAYS?*

**Enjoy your meal.**
Bom apetite!
*bown ah-pay-CHEE-chee!*

**I want this.**
Quero isso aqui.
*KEH-roo EE-soo ah-KEE.*

**Please cook my meat well done.**
Carne bem passada, por favor.
*KAH-nee bayn pah-SAH-da, poer fa-VOER.*

**Please cook my meat medium rare.**
Carne ao ponto, por favor.
*KAH-nee AH-oo PON-too, poer fa-VOER.*

**Please prepare my meat rare.**
Carne mal passada, por favor.
*KAH-nee MAH-oo pah-SAH-da, poer fa-VOER.*

**What type of fish do you serve?**
Que tipo de peixe vocês têm?
*kee CHEE-poo gee PAY-shee voe-SAYS tayn?*

**Can I make a substitution with my meal?**
Posso fazer uma troca no meu prato?
*POH-soo fah-ZAYR OO-ma TROH-ka noo MAY-oo PRAH-too?*

**Do you have a booster seat for my child?**
Tem uma cadeira alta para o meu filho?
*tayn OO-ma ka-DAY-ra AHW-ta PAH-ra oo MAY-oo FEE-lyo?*

**Call us when you get a table.**
Chame a gente quando conseguir uma mesa.
*SHAM-mee ah ZHAIN-chee KWAN-doo kon-say-GHEEH OO-ma MAY-za.*

**Is this a non-smoking section?**
Essa área é para não-fumantes?
*EH-sa AH-rya eh PAH-ra NANN-oo foo-MAHN-chees?*

**We would like to be seated in the smoking section.**
Gostaríamos de sentar na área de fumantes.
*goes-ta-REE-a-moos gee sayn-TAH nah AH-rya gee foo-MAN-chees.*

**This meat tastes funny.**
Essa carne tem um gosto estranho.
*EH-sa KAH-nee tayn oom GOES-too ays-TRAN-gnoo.*

**More people will be joining us later.**
Mais algumas pessoas vão chegar depois.
*MAH-ees ahw-GOOM-as pay-SOE-ahs vawm shay-GAH day-POYS.*

# TRANSPORTATION

**Where's the train station?**
Onde é a estação de trem?
*OWN-gee eh ah ees-tah-SAWM gee trayn?*

**How much does it cost to get to this address?**
Quanto custa para ir até esse endereço?
*KWAN-too KOOS-ta eer ah-TEH AY-see ayn-day-RAY-soo?*

**What type of payment do you accept?**
Que tipo de pagamento você aceita?
*kee CHEE-poo gee pah-gah-MAIN-to voe-SAY ah-SAY-ta?*

**Do you have first-class tickets available?**
Você têm passagens de primeira classe?
*voe-SAY tayn pah-SAH-zhayns gee pree-MAY-ra KLAH-see?*

**What platform do I need to be on to catch this train?**
Preciso ficar em qual plataforma para pegar esse trem?
*pray-SEE-zoo fee-KAR ayn kwaw pla-ta-FOH-ma PAH-ra pay-GAH AY-sy trayn?*

**Are the roads paved in this area?**
As estradas são pavimentadas nessa região?
*ahs ees-TRA-das sawm pah-vee-main-TAH-das NEH-sa hay-zhee-AWM?*

**Where are the dirt roads, and how do I avoid them?**
Onde ficam as estradas ruins, e como eu evito elas?
*OWN-gee FEE-kam ahs ees-TRA-das hoo-EENS, ee KOE-moo AY-oo ay-VEE-too EH-las?*

**Are there any potholes I need to avoid?**
Tem alguma estrada esburacada que eu precise evitar?
*tayn ahw-GOOM-ah ees-TRA-da ays-boo-rah-KAH-da kee AY-oo pray-SEE-zoo ay-VEE-tah?*

70

### How fast are you going?

Em qual velocidade você está indo?

*ayn kwaw vay-lo-see-DAH-gee voe-SAY ees-TAH EEN-doo?*

### Do I need to put my emergency blinkers on?

Preciso ligar meu pisca-pisca?

*pray-SEE-zoo lee-GAH MAY-oo PEES-ka PEES-ka?*

### Make sure to use the right turn signals.

Use o pisca-pisca correto.

*OO-zy oo PEES-ka PEES-ka koe-HEH-too.*

### We need a good mechanic.

Precisamos de um bom mecânico.

*pray-see-ZAM-moos gee oom bowm may-KAN-nee-koo.*

### Can we get a push?

Podem empurrar o carro com a gente?

*POH-dayn ayn-poo-HAH oo KAH-hoo kom ah ZHAIN-chee?*

### I have to call the towing company to move my car.

Preciso ligar para a empresa rebocar o meu carro.

*pray-SEE-zoo lee-GAR PAH-ra ah aim-PRAY-za hay-boe-KAH oo MAY-oo KAH-hoo.*

### Make sure to check the battery and spark plugs for any problems.

Se tiver algum problema, verifique a bateria e a ignição.

*sy chee-VEH ahw-GOOM proe-BLAY-mah, vay-ree-FEE-kee ah bah-tay-REE-a y ah ee-ghee-nee-SAWM.*

### Check the oil level.

Verifique o nível do óleo.

*vay-ree-FEE-kee oo NEE-vew doo OH-lyo.*

### I need to notify my insurance company.

Preciso avisar ao meu seguro.

*pray-SEE-zoo ah-VEE-zah AH-oo MAY-oo say-GOO-roo.*

### When do I pay the taxi driver?

Quando pago o taxista?

*KWAN-doo PAH-goo oo tak-SYS-ta?*

**Please take me to the nearest train station.**
Por favor, me leve para a estação de trem mais próxima.
*poer fa-VOER, mee LEH-vee PAH-ra ah ees-tah-SAWM gee trayn MAH-ees PROH-see-ma.*

**How long does it take to get to this address?**
Quanto tempo demora para chegar nesse endereço?
*KWAN-too TAYM-poo day-MOH-ra PAH-ra shay-GAH NAY-sy ayn-day-RAY-soo?*

**Can you stop here, please?**
Pode parar aqui, por favor?
*POH-gee pa-RAH ah-KEE, poer fa-VOER?*

**You can drop me off anywhere around here.**
Pode me deixar em qualquer lugar por aqui.
*POH-gee mee day-SHAR ayn kwaw-KEHR loo-GAR poor ah-KEE.*

**Is there a charge for extra passengers?**
É mais caro se levarmos outros passageiros?
*eh MAH-ees KAH-roo see lay-VAH-moos OE-troos pah-sah-ZHAY-roos?*

**What is the condition of the road? Is it safe to travel there?**
Quais são as condições da estrada? É seguro viajar por lá?
*KWA-ees sawm ahs kon-gee-SOYS dah ees-TRA-da? Eh say-GOO-roo vee-ah-ZHAH poeh lah?*

**Take me to the emergency room.**
Me leve para o quarto de emergência.
*mee LEH-vee PAH-ra oo KWAR-too gee ay-mayh-ZHAYN-sya.*

**Take me to the embassy.**
Me leve para a embaixada.
*mee LEH-vee PAH-ra ah ayn-bye-SHAH-da.*

**I want to travel around the country.**
Quero viajar pelo país.
*KEH-roo vee-ah-ZHAH PAY-loo pah-EES.*

**Is this the right side of the road?**
Esse é o lado certo da estrada?
*AY-sy eh oo LAH-doo SEH-too dah ees-TRA-da?*

**My car broke down, please help!**
O meu carro quebrou, ajuda por favor!
*oo MAY-oo KAH-hoo kay-BROE, ah-ZHOO-da poer fa-VOER!*

**Can you help me change my tire?**
Pode me ajudar a trocar o pneu?
*POH-gee me ah-zhoo-DAR ah troe-KAH oo pay-NAY-oo?*

**Where can I get a rental car?**
Onde posso alugar um carro?
*OWN-gee POH-soo ah-loo-GAR oom KAH-hoo?*

**Please take us to the hospital.**
Por favor, nos leve para o hospital.
*poer fa-VOER, noos LEH-vee PAH-ra oo oes-py-TAH-oo.*

**Is that the car rental office?**
Essa é a empresa de aluguel de carros?
*EH-sa eh ah aim-PRAY-za gee ah-loo-GHEH-oo gee KAH-hoos?*

**May I have a price list for your fleet?**
Posso ver a lista de preços da frota?
*POH-soo vayh ah LEES-ta gee PRAY-soos dah FROH-ta?*

**Can I get insurance on this rental car?**
Posso ver o seguro desse carro alugado?
*POH-soo vayh oo say-GOO-roo DAY-sy KAH-hoo ah-loo-GAH-doo?*

**How much is the car per day?**
Qual é o preço da diária do carro?
*kwaw eh oo PRAY-soo dah GEE-ahH-rya doo KAH-hoo?*

**How many kilometers can I travel with this car?**
Quantos quilômetros eu posso viajar com esse carro?
*KWAN-toos kee-LOE-meh-troos AY-oo POH-soo vee-ah-ZHAH kom AY-sy KAH-hoo?*

**I would like maps of the region if you have them.**
Gostaria de mapas da região, se tiver.
*goes-ta-REE-a gee MAH-pas dah hay-zhee-AWM, see chee-VEH.*

**When I am done with the car, where do I return it?**
Quando eu terminar de usar o carro, onde eu devolvo?

*KWAN-doo AY-oo tayh-mee-NAH gee oo-ZAR oo KAH-hoo, OWN-gee AY-oo day-VOE-voo?*

**Is this a standard or automatic transmission?**
O carro é manual ou automático?
*oo KAH-hoo eh ma-noo-AHW oe ahw-toe-MAH-chee-koo?*

**Is this car gas-efficient? How many kilometers per liter?**
Esse carro é econômico? Roda quantos quilômetros por litro?
*AY-sy KAH-hoo eh ay-koe-NOE-mee-koo? HOH-da KWAN-toos kee-LOE-meh-troos poeh LEE-tro?*

**Where is the spare tire stored?**
Onde fica o pneu reserva?
*OWN-gee FEE-ka oo pay-NAY-oo hay-ZEH-va?*

**Are there places around the city that are difficult to drive?**
Algum lugar da cidade é mais difícil de dirigir?
*ahw-GOOM loo-GAR da see-DAH-gee eh MAH-ees gy-FEE-seew gee gee-ree-ZHEE?*

**At what time of the day is the traffic the worst?**
Em qual hora do dia o trânsito fica pior?
*ayn kwaw OH-ra doo GEE-ah oo TRAN-zee-too FEE-ka pee-OR?*

**We can't park right here.**
Não podemos estacionar aqui.
*NANN-oo po-DAY-moos ees-ta-see-oe-NAH ah-KEE.*

**What is the speed limit?**
Qual é o limite de velocidade?
*kwaw eh oo lee-MEE-chee gee vay-lo-see-DAH-gee?*

**Keep the change.**
Fique com o troco.
*FEE-ky kom oo TROE-koo.*

**Now let's get off here.**
Agora vamos sair daqui.
*ah-GOH-ra VAM-moos sah-EEH dah-KEE.*

**Where is the train station?**
Onde fica a estação de trem?
*OWN-gee FEE-ka ah ees-tah-SAWM gee trayn?*

**Is the bus stop nearby?**
O ponto de ônibus está perto?
*oo PON-too gee OWN-nee-boos ees-TAH PEH-too?*

**When does the bus run?**
Quando o ônibus vai chegar?
*KWAN-doo oo OWN-nee-boos VAH-ee shay-GAH?*

**Where do I go to catch a taxi?**
Onde eu vou para pegar um táxi?
*OWN-gee AY-oo voe PAH-ra pay-GAH oom TAK-sy?*

**Does the train go to the north station?**
O trem vai para a estação do norte?
*oo trayn VAH-ee PAH-ra ah ees-tah-SAWM doo NOH-chee?*

**Where do I go to purchase tickets?**
Onde eu posso comprar a passagem?
*OWN-gee AY-oo POH-soo kom-PRAH ah pah-SAH-zhayn?*

**How much is a ticket to the north?**
Quanto é a passagem para o norte?
*KWAN-too eh ah pah-SAH-zhayn PAH-ra oo NOH-chee?*

**What is the next stop along this route?**
Qual é a próxima parada nesse percurso?
*kwaw eh ah PROH-see-ma pah-RAH-da NAY-sy payh-KOOH-soo?*

**Can I have a ticket to the north?**
Preciso de uma passagem para o norte.
*pray-SEE-zoo gee OO-ma pah-SAH-zhayn PAH-ra oo NOR-chee.*

**Where is my designated platform?**
Onde fica a minha plataforma?
*OWN-gee FEE-ka ah MEE-nya pla-ta-FOR-ma?*

**Where do I place my luggage?**
Onde eu coloco a minha bagagem?
*OWN-gee AY-oo koe-LOH-koo ah MEE-nya bah-GA-zhayn?*

**Are there any planned closures today?**
Tem algum bloqueio no trânsito hoje?
*tayn ahw-GOOM bloe-KAY-oo noo TRAN-zee-too OE-zhee?*

**Where are the machines that disperse tickets?**
Onde ficam as máquinas das passagens?
*OWN-gee FEE-kam ahs MAH-kee-nas das pah-SAH-zhayns?*

**Does this car come with insurance?**
Esse carro vem com seguro?
*AY-sy KAH-hoo vayn kom say-GOO-roo?*

**May I have a timetable, please?**
Posso ver a tabela de horários, por favor?
*POH-soo vayh ah ta-BEH-la gee oe-RAH-ryos, poer fa-VOER?*

**How often do trains come to this area?**
Com que frequência os trens vêm para essa região?
*kom kee fray-KEWN-sya oos trayns vayn PAH-ra EH-sa hay-zhee-AWM?*

**Is the train running late?**
O trem está atrasado?
*oo trayn ees-TAH ah-tra-ZAH-doo?*

**Has the train been cancelled?**
O trem foi cancelado?
*oo trayn foy kan-say-LAH-doo?*

**Is this seat available?**
Esse assento está disponível?
*AY-sy ah-SAYN-too ees-TAH gees-poe-NEE-vew?*

**Do you mind if I sit here?**
Posso sentar aqui?
*POH-soo sayn-TAH ah-KEE?*

**I've lost my ticket.**
Perdi a minha passagem.
*payh-GEE ah MEE-nya pah-SAH-zhayn.*

**Excuse me, this is my stop.**
Com licença, essa é a minha parada.
*Kom lee-SAIN-sa, EH-sa eh ah MEE-nya pah-RA-da.*

**Can you please open the window?**
Você pode abrir a janela, por favor?
*voe-SAY POH-gee ah-BREEH ah zha-NEH-la, poer fa-VOER?*

**Is smoking allowed in the car?**
Pode fumar nesse carro?
*POH-gee foo-MAH NAY-sy KAH-hoo?*

**Wait, my luggage is still on board!**
Espera, a minha bagagem ainda está lá dentro!
*ees-PEH-ra, ah MEE-nya bah-GAH-zhayn ah-EEN-da ees-TAH lah DAYN-troo!*

**Where can I get a map?**
Onde eu pego um mapa?
*OWN-gee AY-oo PEH-goo oom MAH-pa?*

**What zone is this?**
Que bairro é esse?
*kee BYE-hoo eh AY-sy?*

**Please be careful of the gap!**
Cuidado com a abertura!
*kooy-DAH-doo kom ah ah-bayh-TOO-ra!*

**I am about to run out of gas.**
Estou quase ficando sem combustível.
*ees-TOE KWAH-zee fee-KAN-doo sayn kom-boos-CHEE-vew.*

**My tank is halfway full.**
O meu tanque está metade completo.
*oo MAY-oo TAN-kee ees-TAH may-TAH-gee kom-PLEH-too.*

**What type of gas does this car take?**
Que tipo de combustível funciona com esse carro?
*kee CHEE-poo gee kom-boos-CHEE-vew foon-see-OE-na kom AY-sy KAH-hoo?*

**There is gas leaking out of my car.**
Tem combustível vazando do meu carro.
*tayn kom-boos-CHEE-vew vah-ZAN-doo KAH-hoo.*

**Fill up the tank.**
Enche o tanque.
*AYN-shee oo TAN-kee.*

**There is no more gas in my car.**
Não tem mais combustível no meu carro.
*NANN-oo tayn MAH-ees kom-boos-CHEE-vew noo MAY-oo KAH-hoo.*

**Where can I find the nearest gas station?**
Onde é o posto de combustível mais próximo?
*OWN-gee eh oo POES-too gee kom-boos-CHEE-vew MAH-ees PROH-see-moo?*

**The engine light for my car is on.**
A luz do motor do meu carro está acesa.
*ah loos doo moe-TOEH doo MAY-oo KAH-hoo ees-TAH ah-SAY-za.*

**Do you mind if I drive?**
Posso dirigir?
*POH-soo gee-ree-ZHEE?*

**Please get in the back seat.**
Vá no banco de trás, por favor.
*vah noo BAN-koo gee TRAH-ys poer fa-VOER.*

**Let me get my bags out before you leave.**
Deixa eu tirar a minha bagagem antes de você sair.
*DAY-sha AY-oo chee-RAH ah MEE-nya bah-GAH-zhayn AHN-chees gee voe-SAY sah-EEH.*

**The weather is bad, please drive slowly.**
O tempo está ruim, por favor dirija devagar.
*oo TAYM-poo ees-TAH hoo-EEN, poer fa-VOER gee-REE-zha gee-va-GAH.*

**Our vehicle isn't equipped to travel there.**
O nosso veículo não está preparado para viajar para lá.
*oo NOH-soo vay-EE-koo-loo NANN-oo ees-TAH pray-pah-RA-doo PAH-ra vee-ah-ZHAH PAH-ra lah.*

**One ticket to the north, please.**
Uma passagem para o norte, por favor.
*OO-ma pah-SAH-zhayn PAH-ra oo NOH-chee, poer fa-VOER.*

**If you get lost, call me.**
Se você se perder, me ligue.
*sy voe-SAY see payh-DAYH, mee LEE-ghee.*

**That bus is overcrowded. I will wait for the next one.**
Esse ônibus está lotado. Vou esperar pelo próximo.
*AY-sy OWN-nee-boos ees-TAH loe-TAH-doo. Voe ees-pay-RAH oo PROH-see-moo.*

**Please, take my seat.**
Sente aqui, por favor.
*SAYN-chee ah-KEE, poer fa-VOER.*

**Ma'am, I think your stop is coming up.**
Senhora, acho que a sua parada está chegando.
*sain-GNOH-ra, AH-shoo kee ah SOO-a pa-RA-da ees-TAH shay-GAN-doo.*

**Wake me up when we get to our destination.**
Me acorde quando chegarmos no nosso destino.
*mee ah-KOH-gee KWAN-doo chay-GAH-moos noo NOH-soo days-CHEE-noo.*

**I would like to purchase a travel pass for the entire day.**
Gostaria de comprar um passe de viagem para o dia inteiro.
*goes-ta-REE-a gee kom-PRAH oom PAH-see gee vy-AH-zhayn PAH-ra oo GEE-ah een-TAY-roo.*

**Would you like to swap seats with me?**
Quer trocar de lugar comigo?
*kehr troe-KAH gee loo-GAR ko-MEE-goo?*

**I want to sit with my family.**
Quero sentar com a minha família.
*KEH-roo sayn-TAH kom ah MEE-nya fa-MEE-lya.*

**I would like a window seat for this trip.**
Quero um assento na janela.
*KEH-roo oom ah-SAYN-too nah zha-NEH-la.*

# RELIGIOUS QUESTIONS

**Where can I go to pray?**
Onde posso ir para rezar?
*OWN-gee POH-soo eer PAH-ra hay-ZAH?*

**What services does your church offer?**
Quais são as cerimônias que vocês fazem?
*KWA-ees sawm ahs say-ree-MOE-nyas kee voe-SAYS FAH-zayn?*

**Are you non-denominational?**
Vocês não tem denominação?
*Voe-SAYS NANN-oo tayn day-noe-mee-na-SAWM?*

**Is there a shuttle to your church?**
Tem algum transporte para a sua igreja?
*tayn ahw-GOOM trans-POH-chee PAH-ra ah SOO-a ee-GRAY-zha?*

**How long does church last?**
Quanto tempo dura a cerimônia?
*KWAN-too TAYM-poo DOO-ra ah say-ree-MOE-nya?*

**Where is your bathroom?**
Onde é o banheiro?
*OWN-gee eh oo bahn-GNAY-roo?*

**What should I wear to your services?**
O que devo vestir para a cerimônia?
*oo kee DAY-voo vays-CHEEH PAH-ra ah say-ree-MOE-nya?*

**Where is the nearest Catholic church?**
Onde fica a igreja católica mais próxima?
*OWN-gee FEE-ka ah ee-GRAY-zha MAH-ees PROH-see-ma?*

**Where is the nearest mosque?**
Onde fica a mesquita mais próxima?
*OWN-gee FEE-ka ah mays-KEE-ta MAH-ees PROH-see-ma?*

**Does your church perform weddings?**
A sua igreja celebra casamentos?
*ah SOO-a ee-GRAY-zha say-LEH-bra kah-za-MAIN-toos?*

**Who is getting married?**
Quem está se casando?
*kayn ees-TAH see kah-ZAN-doo?*

**Will our marriage license be legal if we leave the country?**
A nossa licença de casamento vai estar dentro da lei se sairmos do país?
*ah NOH-sa lee-SAIN-sa gee kah-za-MAIN-too VAH-ee ays-TAH DAYN-troo*
*dah lay see sah-EER-moos doo pah-EES?*

**Where do we get our marriage license?**
Onde pegamos a nossa licença de casamento?
*OWN-gee pay-GAM-moos ah NOH-sa lee-SAIN-sa gee kah-za-MAIN-too?*

**What is the charge for marrying us?**
Quanto custa para se casar aqui?
*KWAN-too KOOS-ta PAH-ra see kah-ZAR ah-KEE?*

**Do you handle same-sex marriage?**
Vocês fazem casamento do mesmo sexo?
*voe-SAYS FAH-zayn kah-za-MAIN-too doo MAYS-moo SEH-kso?*

**Please gather here to pray.**
Por favor, se reúnam aqui para rezar.
*poer fa-VOER, see hay-OO-nam ah-KEE PAH-ra hay-ZAH.*

**I would like to lead a sermon.**
Eu gostaria de fazer uma pregação.
*AY-oo goes-ta-REE-a gee fah-ZAYR OO-ma pray-ga-SAWM.*

**I would like to help with prayer.**
Eu gostaria de ajudar com orações.
*AY-oo goes-ta-REE-a gee ah-zhoo-DAR kom oe-ra-SOYS.*

**How should I dress before arriving?**
Como devo me vestir antes de chegar?
*KOE-moo DAY-voo mee vays-CHEEH AHN-chees gee shay-GAH?*

**What are your rules?**
Quais são as regras de vocês?
*KWA-ees sawm ahs HEH-gras gee voe-SAYS?*

**Are cell phones allowed in your building?**
É permitido celular no local?
*eh payr-mee-CHEE-doo say-loo-LAH noo loe-KAW?*

**I plan on bringing my family this Sunday.**
Pretendo trazer a minha família nesse domingo.
*pray-TAYN-doo trah-ZAYH ah MEE-nya fa-MEE-lya NAY-sy doo-MEEN-goo.*

**Do you accept donations?**
Vocês aceitam doações?
*voe-SAYS ah-SAY-tam doe-ah-SOYS?*

**I would like to offer my time to your cause.**
Eu gostaria de me oferecer para a causa de vocês.
*AY-oo goes-ta-REE-a gee mee oe-fay-ray-SAYH PAH-ra ah KAW-za gee voe-SAYS.*

**What book should I be reading from?**
A partir de qual livro eu devo ler?
*ah pah-CHEER gee kwaw LEE-vro AY-oo DAY-voo layh?*

**Do you have a gift store?**
Vocês têm uma loja de presentes?
*voe-SAYS tayn OO-ma LOH-zha gee pray-ZAYN-chees?*

# EMERGENCY

**I need help over here!**
Preciso de ajuda aqui!
*pray-SEE-zoo gee ah-ZHOO-da ah-KEE!*

**I'm lost, please help me.**
Estou perdido, me ajude, por favor.
*ees-TOE peh-GEE-doo, mee ah-ZHOO-gee poer fa-VOER.*

**Someone call the police!**
Alguém chame a polícia!
*AHW-gain SHAM-mee ah poe-LEE-cya!*

**Is there a lawyer who speaks English?**
Tem um advogado que fala inglês?
*tayn oom ah-gee-voe-GAH-doo kee FAH-la een-GLAYS?*

**Please help, my car doesn't work.**
Ajuda, por favor, o meu carro não está funcionando.
*ah-ZHOO-da, poer fa-VOER, oo MAY-oo KAH-hoo NANN-oo ees-TAH foon-see-OE-nan-doo.*

**There was a collision!**
O carro bateu!
*oo KAH-hoo bah-TAY-oo!*

**Call an ambulance!**
Chame uma ambulância!
*SHAM-mee OO-ma am-boo-LAN-sya!*

**Am I under arrest?**
Estou preso?
*ees-TOE PRAY-zoo?*

**I need an interpreter, this is an emergency!**
Preciso de um intérprete, é uma emergência!

*pray-SEE-zoo gee oom een-TEH-pray-chee, eh OO-ma ay-mayh-ZHAYN-sya!*

**My back hurts.**
Minhas costas estão doendo.
*MEE-nyas KOHS-tas ees-TAWM doe-AIN-doo.*

**Is there an American consulate here?**
Tem um consulado americano aqui?
*tayn oom kon-soo-LAH-doo ah-may-ree-KAN-noo ah-KEE?*

**I'm sick and don't feel too well.**
Estou doente e não me sinto muito bem.
*ees-TOE doe-AIN-chee y NANN-oo mee SEEN-too MOON-ee-too bayn.*

**Is there a pharmacy where I can get medicine?**
Tem uma farmácia onde eu possa comprar remédio?
*tayn OO-ma fah-MAH-cya OWN-gee AY-oo POH-sa kom-PRAH hay-MEH-gyo?*

**I need a doctor immediately.**
Preciso de um médico imediatamente.
*pray-SEE-zoo gee oom MEH-gee-koo ee-may-GEE-ahh-ta-MAYN-chee.*

**I have a tooth missing.**
Estou sem um dente.
*ees-TOE sain oom DAYN-chee.*

**Please! Someone bring my child to me!**
Alguém pode trazer o meu filho, por favor?
*AHW-gain POH-gee trah-ZAYH oo MAY-oo FEE-lyo, poer fa-VOER?*

**Where does it hurt?**
Onde está doendo?
*OWN-gee ees-TAH doe-AIN-doo?*

**Hold on to me!**
Segure em mim!
*say-GOO-ree ayn meen!*

**There's an emergency!**
É uma emergência!
*eh OO-ma ay-mayh-ZHAYN-sya!*

**I need a telephone to call for help.**
Preciso de um telefone para pedir ajuda.
*pray-SEE-zoo gee oom tay-lay-FOE-nee PAH-ra pay-GEEH ah-ZHOO-da.*

**My nose is bleeding.**
O meu nariz está sangrando.
*oo MAY-oo nah-REES ees-TAH san-GRAN-doo.*

**I twisted my ankle.**
Torci o meu tornozelo.
*toeh-SEE oo MAY-oo toeh-noe-ZAY-loo.*

**I don't feel so good.**
Não estou me sentindo muito bem.
*NANN-oo ees-TOE me sain-TEEN-doo MOON-ee-too bayn.*

**Don't move, please.**
Não se mexa, por favor.
*NANN-oo see MAY-sha, poer fa-VOER.*

**Hello operator, can I place a collect call?**
Oi, posso fazer uma chamada a cobrar?
*OE-y, POH-soo fah-ZAYR OO-ma sha-MA-da ah koe-BRAH?*

**I'll get a doctor for you.**
Vou chamar um médico.
*voe sha-MAH oom MEH-gee-koo.*

**Please hold my passports for a while.**
Por favor, segure o meu passaporte por um momento.
*poer fa-VOER, say-GOO-ree moe-MAIN-too.*

**I lost my wallet.**
Perdi a minha carteira.
*ah MEE-nya.*

**I have a condition! Please check my wallet.**
Estou doente! Por favor, dê uma olhada na minha carteira.
*ees-TOE doe-AIN-chee poer fa-VOER deh OO-ma oe-LYA-da nah MEE-nya car-TAY-ra.*

**My wife is in labor, please help!**
Minha esposa está em trabalho de parto, me ajude por favor!

*MEE-nya ees-POE-za ees-TAH ayn trah-BAH-lyo gee PAH-too, mee ah-ZHOO-gee poer fa-VOER!*

**I would like to talk to my lawyer.**
Eu gostaria de falar com o meu advogado.
*goes-ta-REE-a gee fah-LAR kom oo MAY-oo ah-gee-voe-GAH-doo.*

**It's an earthquake!**
É um terremoto!
*Es ist ighn AYRD-bay-ben!*

**Get under the desk and protect your head.**
Fique embaixo da mesa e proteja a sua cabeça.
*FEE-ky ain-BYE-shoo dah MAY-za y ah SOO-a ka-BAY-sa.*

**How can I help you?**
Como posso te ajudar?
*KOE-moo POH-soo ah-zhoo-DAR?*

**Everyone, he needs help!**
Pessoal, ele está precisando de ajuda!
*AY-ly ees-TAH prAY-sy-zan-doo!*

**Yes, help me get an ambulance.**
Sim, me ajude a chamar uma ambulância.
*seem, mee ah-ZHOO-gee ah sha-MAH OO-ma am-boo-LAN-sya.*

**Thank you, but I am fine. Please don't help me.**
Obrigado, estou bem. Não estou precisando de ajuda.
*oe-bree-GAH-doo, ees-TOE bayn. NANN-oo ees-TOE prAY-sy-ZAN-doo gee ah-ZHOO-da.*

**I need help carrying this injured person.**
Preciso de ajuda para levar essa pessoa machucada.
*pray-SEE-zoo gee ah-ZHOO-da PAH-ra lay-VAH EH-sa pay-SOE-ah mah-SHOE-kah-dah.*

# TECHNOLOGY

**What is the country's official website?**
Qual é o site oficial do país?
*kwaw eh oo SAH-ee-chee oe-fee-see-AHW doo pah-EES?*

**Do you know the name of a good wi-fi café?**
Você conhece algum café com wi-fi?
*Voe-SAY koe-GNEH-see ahw-GOOM ka-FEH kom wi-fi?*

**Do you have any experience with computers?**
Você tem experiência com computadores?
*voe-SAY tayn ays-pay-ree-AYN-sya kom kom-poo-ta-DOE-rys?*

**How well do you know Apple products?**
Você conhece bem os produtos da Apple?
*voe-SAY koe-NYEH-see bayn oos proe-DOO-toos dah Apple?*

**What kind of work did you do with computers?**
Que tipo de trabalho você já fez com computador?
*kee CHEE-poo gee trah-BAH-lyo voe-SAY zha fays skom kom-poo-ta-DOEH?*

**Are you a programmer?**
Você é programador?
*voe-SAY eh proe-gram-mah-DOEH?*

**Are you a developer?**
Você é desenvolvedor?
*voe-SAY eh day-zayn-voe-vay-DOEH?*

**I want to use this computer instead of that one.**
Quero usar esse computador, e não aquele.
*KEH-roo oo-ZAR AY-sy kom-poo-tah-DOEH, y NANN-oo ah-KAY-ly.*

**Do you know where I can buy discount computer parts?**
Você sabe onde eu posso comprar peças de computador baratas?

*voe-SAY SAH-bee OWN-gee AY-oo POH-soo kom-PRAH PEH-sas gee kom-poo-ta-DOEH bah-RAH-tas?*

**I have ten years of experience with Windows.**
Tenho dez anos de experiência com Windows.
*TAYN-gnoo DEH-ysANN-noosgee ays-pay-ree-AYN-sya kom Windows.*

**What is the wi-fi password?**
Qual é a senha do wi-fi?
*kwaw eh ah SAYN-gna doo wi-fi?*

**I need to have my login information reset.**
Preciso redefinir os dados do meu login.
*pray-SEE-zoo hay-day-fee-NEEH oos DAH-doos doo MAY-oo loe-GHEEN.*

**The hard drive is making a clicking noise.**
O disco rígido está fazendo barulho de clique.
*oo GEES-koo HEE-zhee-doo ees-TAH fah-ZAIN-doo bah-ROO-lyo gee KLEE-ky.*

**How do I uninstall this program from my device?**
Como desinstalar esse programa do meu aparelho?
*KOE-moo days-eens-tah-LAH AY-sy proe-GRAM-ma doo MAY-oo ah-pah-RAY-lyo?*

**Can you help me set up a new account with this website?**
Você pode me ajudar a criar uma conta nova nesse site?
*voe-SAY POH-gee mee ah-zhoo-DAR ah kree-AH OO-ma KON-ta NOH-va NAY-sy SAH-ee-chee?*

**Why is the internet so slow?**
Por que a internet está tão lenta?
*poor-KAY ah een-tayh-NEH-chee ees-TAH tawm LAYN-ta?*

**Why is YouTube buffering every video I play?**
Por que o YouTube está fazendo buffering de todos os vídeos que eu abro?
*poor-KAY oo you TOO-bee ees-TAH fah-ZAIN-doo buffering gee TOE-doos oos VEE-gee-oos kee AY-oo AH-broo?*

**My web camera isn't displaying a picture.**
A minha webcam não está funcionando.
*ah MEE-nya webcam NANN-oo ees-TAH foon-see-OE-nan-doo.*

**I have no bars on my phone.**
O meu celular está sem conexão.
*oo MAY-oo say-LOO-lah ees-TAH sayn koe-nayk-SAWM.*

**Where can I get my phone serviced?**
Onde eu posso consertar o meu celular?
*OWN-gee AY-oo POH-soo kon-say-TAH oo MAY-oo say-LOO-lah?*

**My phone shows that it is charging but won't charge.**
O meu celular mostra que está carregando, mas não carrega.
*oo MAY-oo say-LOO-lah MOHS-tra kee ees-TAH ka-hay-GAN-doo, MAH-ees NANN-oo ka-HEH-ga.*

**I think someone else is controlling my computer.**
Acho que outra pessoa está controlando o meu computador.
*AH-shoo kee OE-tra pay-SOE-ah ees-TAH kon-troe-LAN-doo oo MAY-oo kom-poo-ta-DOEH.*

**My computer just gave a blue screen and shut down.**
O meu computador só mostrou uma tela azul e desligou.
*oo MAY-oo kom-poo-ta-DOEH soh moes-TROE OO-ma THE-la ah-ZOO y days-lee-GOE.*

**Do you have the battery for this laptop?**
Você tem bateria para esse notebook?
*voe-SAY tayn bah-tay-REE-a PAH-ra AY-sy noe-chee-BOO-ky?*

**Where can I get a compatible adapter?**
Onde posso comprar uma fonte compatível?
*OWN-gee POH-soo kom-PRAH OO-ma FON-chee kom-pah-CHEE-vew?*

**I can't get online with the information you gave me.**
Não consigo ficar online com as informações que você me passou.
*NANN-oo kon-SEE-goo fee-KAR on-LAH-y-nee kom as een-foeh-mah-SONN-ees kee voe-SAY mee pah-SOE.*

**This keyboard is not working correctly.**
Esse teclado não está funcionando direito.
*AY-sy tay-KLAH-doo NANN-oo ees-TAH foon-see-oe-NAN-doo gee-RAY-too.*

**What is the login information for this computer?**
Quais são as informações de login desse computador?

*KWA-ees sawm ahs een-foeh-mah-SONN-ees gee loe-GHEEN DAY-sy kom-poo-ta-DOEH?*

**I need you to update my computer.**
Atualize o meu computador, por favor.
*ah-too-ah-LEE-zee oo MAY-oo kom-poo-ta-DOEH, poer fa-VOER.*

**Can you build my website?**
Você pode fazer o meu site?
*voe-SAY POH-gee fah-ZAYR oo MAY-oo SAH-ee-chee?*

**I prefer Wordpress.**
Prefiro Wordpress.
*pray-FEE-roo Wordpress.*

**What are your rates per hour?**
Quanto você cobra por hora?
*KWAN-too voe-SAY KOH-bra poor OH-ra?*

**Do you have experience handling email servers?**
Você já mexeu com servidor de email?
*voe-SAY zha may-SHAY-oo kom sayh-vee-DOEH gee ee-MAY-oo?*

**I am locked out of my account, can you help?**
Não consigo entrar na minha conta, você pode me ajudar?
*NANN-oo kon-SEE-goo ayn-TRAH nah MEE-nya KON-ta, voe-SAY POH-gee mee ah-zhoo-DAR?*

**None of the emails I am sending are going through.**
Nenhum dos emails que eu estou enviando está chegando.
*nain-GNOOM doos ee-MAY-oos kee AY-oo ees-TOE ain-vee-AN-doo ees-TAH shay-GAN-doo.*

**The time and date on my computer are wrong.**
A data e a hora do meu computador estão incorretas.
*ah DAH-ta y ah OH-ra doo MAY-oo kom-poo-ta-DOEH ees-TAWM en-koe-HEH-tas.*

**Is this game free to play?**
Esse jogo é gratuito?
*AY-sy ZHOE-goo eh gra-TOOY-too?*

**Where do I go to download the client?**
Onde eu faço o download do client?
*OWN-gee AY-oo FAH-soo oo download doo client?*

**I am having trouble chatting with my family.**
Não estou conseguindo conversar com a minha família.
*NANN-oo ees-TOE kon-say-GHEEN-doo kon-vayh-SAH kom ah MEE-nya fa-MEE-lya.*

**Is this the fastest computer here?**
Esse é o computador mais rápido daqui?
*AY-sy eh oo kom-poo-ta-DOEH MAH-ees HAH-pee-doo dah-KEE?*

**How much space is on the computer?**
Quanto de espaço tem no computador?
*KWAN-too gee ees-PAH-soo tayn noo kom-poo-ta-DOEH?*

**Will my profile be deleted once I log out? Or does it save?**
O meu perfil vai ser apagado quando eu sair? Ou vai ficar salvo?
*oo MAY-oo payh-FEEW VAH-ee sayh ah-pah-GAH-doo KWAN-doo AY-oo sah-EEH? oe VAH-ee fee-KAR SAH-oo-voo?*

**How much do you charge for computer use?**
Quanto você cobra para o uso do computador?
*KWAN-too voe-SAY KOH-bra PAH-ra oo OO-zoo doo kom-poo-ta-DOEH?*

**Are group discounts offered?**
Tem desconto para grupos?
*tayn diss-KON-too PAH-ra GROO-poos?*

**Can I use my own headphones with your computer?**
Posso usar o meu próprio fone no seu computador?
*POH-soo oo-ZAR oo MAY-oo PROH-pree-oo FOE-nee noo SAY-oo kom-poo-ta-DOEH?*

**Do you have a data cap?**
Você tem limite de dados?
*voe-SAY tayn lee-MEE-chee gee DAH-doos?*

**I think this computer has a virus.**
Acho que esse computador está com vírus.
*AH-shoo kee AY-sy kom-poo-ta-DOEH ees-TAH kom VEE-roos.*

**The battery for my laptop is running low.**
A bateria do meu notebook está quase acabando.
*ah bah-tay-REE-a doo MAY-oo noe-chee-BOO-ky ees-TAH KWAH-zee ah-ka-BAN-doo.*

**Where can I plug this in? I need to recharge my device.**
Onde eu posso conectar isso? Preciso recarregar o meu aparelho.
*OWN-gee AY-oo POH-soo koe-nayk-TAH EE-soo? pray-SEE-zoo hay-kah-hay-GAH oo MAY-oo ah-pah-RAY-lyo.*

**Do you have a mini-USB cord?**
Você tem um mini conector de USB?
*voe-SAY tayn oom MEE-nee koe-nayk-TOEH gee oo-eh-see-BAY?*

**Where can I go to watch the game?**
Onde eu posso ir para assistir o jogo?
*OWN-gee AY-oo POH-soo eer PAH-ra ah-sees-CHEEH oo ZHOE-goo?*

**Do you have an iPhone charger?**
Você tem carregador de iPhone?
*voe-SAY tayn kah-hay-gah-DOEH gee ah-ee-FOE-nee?*

**I need a new battery for my watch.**
Preciso de uma bateria nova para o meu relógio.
*pray-SEE-zoo gee OO-ma bah-tay-REE-a NOH-va PAH-ra oo MAY-oo hay-LOH-zhee-oo.*

**I need to borrow an HDMI cord.**
Preciso pegar emprestado um cabo HDMI.
*pray-SEE-zoo pay-GAH ayn-prays-TAH-doo oom KAH-boo ah-gah-day-ay-mee-EE.*

**What happens when I exceed the data cap?**
O que acontece se eu exceder o limite de dados?
*oo kee ah-kon-TEH-see see AY-oo ay-say-DAYH oo lee-MEE-chee gee DAH-doos?*

**Can you help me pair my Bluetooth device?**
Você pode me ajudar a conectar o meu dispositivo Bluetooth?
*voe-SAY POH-gee mee ah-zhoo-DAR ah koe-nayk-TAH oo MAY-oo gees-poe-zee-CHEE-voo bloo-TOO-fee?*

**I need a longer ethernet cord.**
Preciso de um cabo de internet mais longo.
*pray-SEE-zoo gee oom KAH-boo gee een-tayh-NEH-chee MAH-ees LON-goo.*

**Why is this website restricted?**
Por que esse site está bloqueado?
*poor-KAY AY-sy SAH-ee-chee ees-TAH bloe-kee-AH-doo?*

**How can I unblock this website?**
Como posso desbloquear esse site?
*KOE-moo POH-soo days-bloe-kee-AH AY-sy SAH-ee-chee?*

**Is that television 4k or higher?**
Essa TV tem resolução maior do que 4k?
*EH-sa tay-VAY tayn hay-zoe-loo-SAWM mah-ee-OHR doo kee KWAH-troo kah?*

**Do you have the Office suite on this computer?**
Esse computador tem o Office instalado?
*AY-sy kom-poo-ta-DOEH tayn oo OH-fee-see yns-tah-LAH-doo?*

**This application won't install on my device.**
Não estou conseguindo instalar esse aplicativo no meu aparelho.
*NANN-oo ees-TOE kon-say-GHEEN-doo eens-tah-LAH AY-sy ah-plee-kah-CHEE-voo noo MAY-oo ah-pah-RAY-lyo.*

**Can you change the channel on the television?**
Você pode mudar o canal na TV?
*voe-SAY POH-gee moo-DAR oo ka-NAW nah tay-VAY?*

**I think a fuse blew.**
Acho que queimou um fusível.
*AH-shoo kee KAY-moe oom foo-ZEE-veal.*

**The screen is black and won't come on.**
A tela está preta e não quer acender.
*ah TEH-la ees-TAH PRAY-ta y NANN-oo kehr ah-SAIN-deh.*

**I keep getting pop-ups on every website.**
Os sites ficam abrindo muitas janelas de pop-up.
*oos SAH-ee-chees FEE-kam ah-BRIN-doo MOON-ee-tas zha-NEH-las gee pop-up.*

**This computer is moving much slower than it should.**
O computador está muito mais lento do que deveria.
*oo kom-poo-ta-DOEH ees-TAH MOON-ee-too MAH-ees LAYN-too doo kee day-vay-RI-a.*

**I need to reactivate my copy of Windows.**
Preciso reativar o Windows.
*pray-SEE-zoo hay-ah-chee-VAH oo oo-EEN-does.*

**Why is this website blocked on my laptop?**
Por que este site está bloqueado no meu notebook?
*poor-KAY AY-sy SAH-ee-chee ees-TAH bloe-kee-AH-doo noo MAY-oo noe-chee-BOO-ky?*

**Can you show me how to download videos to my computer?**
Você pode me mostrar como baixar vídeos para o meu computador?
*voe-SAY POH-gee mee moes-TRAH KOE-moo bye-SHAR VEE-gee-oos PAH-ra oo MAY-oo kom-poo-ta-DOEH?*

**Can I insert a flash drive into this computer?**
Posso colocar um pen drive nesse computador?
*POH-soo koe-loe-KAH oom* pen drive *NAY-sy kom-poo-ta-DOEH?*

**I want to change computers.**
Quero trocar de computador.
*KEH-roo troe-KAH gee kom-poo-ta-DOEH.*

**Is Chrome the only browser I can use with this computer?**
O Chrome é o único navegador que eu posso usar nesse computador?
*oo KROE-mee eh oo OO-ny-koo nah-vay-gah-DOEH kee AY-oo POH-soo oo-ZAR NAY-sy kom-poo-ta-DOEH?*

**Do you track my usage on any of these devices?**
Você rastreia a minha atividade em algum desses aparelhos?
*voe-SAY has-TRAY-ah ah MEE-nya ah-chee-vee-DAH-gee ayn ahw-GOOM DAY-sys ah-pah-RAY-lyos?*

# CONVERSATION TIPS

**Pardon me.**
Me desculpa.
*mee gees-KOO-pa.*

**Please speak more slowly.**
Por favor, fale mais devagar.
*poer fa-VOER, FAH-ly MAH-ees gee-va-GAH.*

**I don't understand.**
Não estou entendendo.
*NANN-oo ees-TOE ain-tayn-DAIN-doo.*

**Can you say that more clearly?**
Você pode dizer isso de forma mais clara?
*voe-SAY POH-gee gee-ZAYR EE-soo gee FOH-ma MAH-ees KLAH-rah?*

**I don't speak Spanish very well.**
Não falo espanhol muito bem.
*NANN-oo FAH-loo ays-pan-GNOH-oo MOON-ee-too bayn.*

**Can you please translate that to English for me?**
Por favor, você pode traduzir para o inglês?
*poer fa-VOER, voe-SAY POH-gee tra-doo-ZEEH PAH-ra oo een-GLAYS?*

**Let's talk over there where it is quieter.**
Vamos conversar ali, está mais calmo.
*VAM-moos kon-vayh-SAH ah-LEE, ees-TAH MAH-ees KAHW-moo.*

**Sit down over there.**
Senta ali.
*SAYN-ta ah-LEE.*

**May I?**
Posso?
*POH-soo?*

**I am from America.**
Sou dos Estados Unidos.
*soe doos ays-TAH-doos oo-NEE-doos.*

**Am I talking too much?**
Estou falando demais?
*ees-TOE fah-LAN-doo gee-MAYS?*

**I speak your language badly.**
Falo mal o seu idioma.
*FAH-loo MAH-oo oo SAY-oo ee-gee-OE-ma.*

**Am I saying that word correctly?**
Estou falando essa palavra do jeito certo?
*ees-TOE fah-LAN-doo EH-sa pah-LAH-vra doo ZHAY-to SEH-too?*

**You speak English very well.**
Você fala inglês muito bem.
*Voe-SAY FAH-la een-GLAYS MOON-ee-too bayn.*

**This is my first time in your lovely country.**
É a minha primeira vez no seu país maravilhoso.
*eh ah MEE-nya pree-MAY-ra vays noo SAY-oo pah-EES mah-rah-VEE-lyoe-zoo.*

**Write that information down on this piece of paper.**
Escreve isso aqui nesse pedaço de papel.
*ees-KREH-vee EE-soo ah-KEE NAY-sy pah-PEHW.*

**Do you understand?**
Você está entendendo?
*voe-SAY ees-TAH ain-tayn-DAIN-doo?*

**How do you pronounce that word?**
Como pronuncio essa palavra?
*KOE-moo proe-noon-SEE-oo EH-sa pah-LAH-vra?*

**Is this how you write this word?**
É assim que se escreve essa palavra?
*eh ah-SEEM kee see ees-KREH-vee EH-sa pah-LAH-vra?*

**Can you give me an example?**
Você pode me dar um exemplo?
*voe-SAY POH-gee mee dah oom ay-ZAYN-loo?*

**Wait a moment, please.**
Espera um momento, por favor.
*ees-PEH-ra oom moe-MAIN-too, poer fa-VOER.*

**If there is anything you want, tell me.**
Se você quiser alguma coisa, me avise.
*see voe-SAY kee-ZEH ahw-GOOM-ah KOY-za, mee ah-VEE-zee.*

**I don't want to bother you anymore, so I will go.**
Não quero mais te incomodar, então vou embora.
*NANN-oo KEH-roo MAH-ees chee een-koe-moe-DAH, ayn-TAWM voe ayn-BOH-ra.*

**Please take care of yourself.**
Se cuida.
*see KOOY-da.*

**When you arrive, let us know**.
Avisa quando chegar.
*ah-VEE-za KWAN-doo shay-GAH.*

# DATE NIGHT

**What is your telephone number?**
Qual é o número do seu telefone?
*kwaw eh oo NOO-may-roo doo SAY-oo tay-lay-FOE-nee?*

**I'll call you for the next date.**
Vou te ligar para nos encontrarmos de novo.
*voe chee lee-GAR PAH-ra noos ayn-kon-TRAH-moos gee NOE-voo.*

**I had a good time, can't wait to see you again.**
Gostei muito, mal posso esperar para te ver de novo.
*goes-TAY MOON-ee-too, MAH-oo POH-soo ays-pay-RAH PAH-ra chee vayh gee NOE-voo.*

**I'll pay for dinner tonight.**
Vou pagar o jantar hoje à noite.
*voe pa-GAH oo zhan-TAH OE-zhee ah NOY-chee.*

**Dinner at my place?**
Janta aqui comigo?
*ZHAN-ta ah-KEE ko-MEE-goo?*

**I don't think we should see each other anymore.**
Acho que a gente não deve mais se ver.
*AH-shoo kee ah ZHAIN-chee NANN-oo DEH-vee MAH-ees see vayh.*

**I'm afraid this will be the last time we see each other.**
Talvez essa seja a última vez que a gente se vê.
*tahw-VAYS EH-sa SAY-zha ah OO-chee-ma vays kee ah ZHAIN-chee see vay.*

**You look fantastic.**
Você está linda (when talking to a woman) | Você está lindo (when talking to a man).
*voe-SAY ees-TAH LEEN-da (to a woman) | voe-SAY ees-TAH LEEN-do (to a man).*

**Would you like to dance with me?**
Quer dançar comigo?
*kehr dan-SAH ko-MEE-goo?*

**Are there any 3D cinemas in this city?**
Tem algum cinema 3D na cidade?
*tayn ahw-GOOM see-NAY-ma trays day nah see-DAH-gee?*

**We should walk along the beach.**
Vamos caminhar na praia.
*VAM-moos ka-mee-NYAR nah PRAH-ya.*

**I hope you like my car.**
Espero que você goste do meu carro.
*Ays-PEH-roo kee voe-SAY GOHS-chee doo MAY-oo KAH-hoo.*

**What movies are playing today?**
Quais filmes estão passando hoje?
*KWA-ees FEEW-mees ees-TAWM pah-SAN-doo OE-zhee?*

**I've seen this film, but I wouldn't mind watching it again.**
Já vi esse filme, mas não me importaria de assistir de novo.
*zha vee AY-sy FEEW-mee, MAH-ees NANN-oo mee eem-poh-tah-REE-a gee
ah-sees-CHEEH gee NOE-voo.*

**Do you know how to do the salsa?**
Você sabe dançar salsa?
*voe-SAY SAH-bee dan-SAH SAHW-sa?*

**We can dance all night.**
Podemos dançar a noite toda.
*po-DAY-moos dan-SAH ah NOY-chee TOE-da.*

**I have some friends that will be joining us tonight.**
Tenho alguns amigos que vão vir hoje à noite.
*TAYN-gnoo ahw-GOON-s ah-MEE-goos kee vawm veeh OE-zhee ah NOY-
chee.*

**Is this a musical or a regular concert?**
Esse é um musical ou um show normal?
*AY-sy eh oom moo-zee-KAHW oe oom show nor-MAHW?*

**Did you get VIP tickets?**
Você comprou ingressos VIP?
*Voe-SAY kom-PROE een-GREH-soos VEE-pee?*

**I'm going to have to cancel on you tonight. Maybe another time?**
Vou precisar cancelar o encontro de hoje. Vamos deixar para outro dia?
*voe pray-see-ZAR kan-say-LAH oo ayn-KON-troo gee OE-zhee. VAM-moos day-SHAR PAH-ra OE-troo GEE-ahh?*

**If you want, we can go to your place.**
Se você quiser, podemos ir para a sua casa.
*see voe-SAY kee-ZEH, po-DAY-moos eer PAH-ra ah SOO-a KAH-za.*

**I'll pick you up tonight.**
Vou te buscar hoje à noite.
*voe chee boos-KAH OE-zhee ah NOY-chee.*

**This one is for you!**
Esse é pra você!
*AY-sy eh prah voe-SAY!*

**What time does the party start?**
Que horas começa a festa?
*kee OH-ras koe-MEH-sa ah FEHS-tah?*

**Will it end on time or will you have to leave early?**
Vai terminar na hora ou você vai ter que sair mais cedo?
*VAH-ee tayh-mee-NAH nah OH-ra oe voe-SAY VAH-ee sah-EEH MAH-ees SAY-doo?*

**Did you like your gift?**
Gostou do presente?
*goes-TOE doo pray-ZAYN-chee?*

**I want to invite you to watch a movie with me tonight.**
Quer assistir um filme comigo hoje à noite?
*kehr ah-sees-CHEEH oom FEEW-mee ko-MEE-goo OE-zhee ah NOY-chee?*

**Do you want anything to drink?**
Quer alguma coisa pra beber?
*kehr ahw-GOOM-ah KOY-za prah bay-BAYH?*

**I am twenty-six years old.**
Tenho vinte e seis anos.
*TAYN-gnoo VEEN-chee y SAY-s ANN-noos.*

**You're invited to a small party I'm having at my house.**
Quero te convidar para uma festinha que vou dar na minha casa.
*KEH-roo kee kon-vee-DAH PAH-ra OO-ma fehs-CHEE-nya kee AY-oo voe dah nah MEE-nya KAH-za.*

**I love you.**
Eu te amo.
*AY-oo chee AH-moo.*

**We should go to the arcade.**
Vamos em uma sala de jogos?
*VAM-moos ayn OO-ma SAH-la gee ZHOH-goos?*

**Have you ever played this game before?**
Você já jogou esse jogo?
*voe-SAY zha ZHOE-goe AY-sy ZHOE-goo?*

**Going on this ferry would be really romantic.**
Andar de balsa seria muito romântico.
*an-DAH gee BAH-oo-sa say-REE-a MOON-ee-too hoe-MAN-chee-koo.*

**How about a candlelight dinner?**
O que acha de um jantar à luz de velas?
*oo kee AH-sha gee oom zhan-TAH ah LOO-ys gee VEH-las?*

**Let's dance and sing!**
Vamos dançar e cantar!
*VAM-moos dan-SAH y kan-TAH!*

**Will you marry me?**
Quer casar comigo?
*kehr kah-ZAR ko-MEE-goo?*

**Set the table, please.**
Arruma a mesa, por favor.
*ah-ROO-mee ah MAY-za, poer fa-VOER.*

**Here are the dishes and the glasses.**
Aqui estão os pratos e os copos.
*ah-KEE ees-TAWM oos PRAH-toos y oos KOH-poos.*

**Where is the cutlery?**
Onde estão os talheres?
*OWN-gee ees-TAWM oos tah-LYEH-rys?*

**May I hold your hand?**
Posso segurar a sua mão?
*POH-soo say-goo-RAH ah SOO-a mawm?*

**Let me get that for you.**
Deixa eu pegar pra você.
*DAY-sha AY-oo pay-GAH prah voe-SAY.*

**I think our song is playing!**
Acho que tá tocando a nossa música!
*AH-shoo kee tah toe-KAN-doo ah NOH-sa MOO-zee-ka!*

**Let's make a wish together.**
Vamos fazer um pedido juntos.
*VAM-moos fah-ZAYR oom pay-GEE-doo ZHOON-toos.*

**Is there anything that you want from me?**
Você quer me pedir alguma coisa?
*voe-SAY kehr mee pay-GEEH ahw-GOOM-ah KOY-za?*

**There is nowhere I would rather be than right here with you.**
Não tem lugar melhor no mundo agora do que aqui com você.
*NANN-oo tayn loo-GAR may-LYOR noo MOON-doo ah-GOH-ra doo kee ah-KEE kom voe-SAY.*

**I'll give you a ride back to your place.**
Vou te levar em casa.
*voe chee lay-VAH ayn KAH-za.*

**Would you like me to hold your purse?**
Quer que eu segure a sua bolsa?
*kehr kee AY-oo say-GOO-ree ah SOO-a BOE-sa?*

**Let's pray before we eat our meal.**
Vamos rezar antes de comer.
*VAM-moos hay-ZAH AHN-chees gee koe-MEHR.*

**Do you need a napkin?**
Quer um guardanapo?
*kehr oom guah-da-NAH-poo?*

**I'm thirsty.**
Estou com sede.
*ees-TOE kom SAY-gee.*

**I hope you enjoy your meal.**
Espero que você goste da comida.
*Ays-PEH-roo kee voe-SAY GOHS-chee dah koe-MEE-da.*

**I need to add more salt to the salt shaker.**
Por favor, coloque mais sal no saleiro.
*poer fa-VOER, koe-LOH-kee MAH-ees SAH-oo noo sah-LAY-roo.*

**We should get married!**
A gente deveria se casar!
*ah ZHAIN-chee day-vay-REE-a see kah-ZAR!*

**How old are you?**
Quantos anos você tem?
*KWAN-toos ANN-nos voe-SAY tayn?*

**Will you dream of me?**
Vai sonhar comigo?
*VAH-ee soe-GNAH ko-MEE-goo?*

**Thank you very much for the wonderful date last night.**
Obrigado pelo encontro maravilhoso de ontem à noite.
*oe-bree-GAH-doo PAY-loo ayn-KON-troo mah-rah-VEE-lyoe-zoo gee OWN-tayn ah NOY-chee.*

**Would you like to come to a party this weekend?**
Quer ir a uma festa nesse final de semana?
*kehr eer ah OO-ma FEHS-tah NAY-sy fy-NAW gee say-MANN-na?*

**This Saturday night, right?**
Sábado à noite, né?
*SAH-ba-doo ah NOY-chee, neh?*

**I will be lonely without you.**
Vou ficar sozinho sem você. (masc.) | Vou ficar sozinha sem você. (fem.)
*voe fee-KAR soh-ZEE-nyo sayn voe-SAY. | voe fee-KAR soh-ZEE-nya sayn voe-SAY.*

**Please stay the night.**
Por favor, passa a noite aqui.
*poer fa-VOER, PAH-sa ah NOY-chee ah-KEE.*

**I like your fragrance.**
Gostei do seu perfume.
*goes-TAY doo SAY-oo payh-FOO-mee.*

**That is a beautiful outfit you're wearing.**
Você está linda com essa roupa. (to a woman) | Você está lindo com essa roupa. (to a man)
*voe-SAY ees-TAH LEEN-da kom EH-sa HOE-pa (to a woman). | voe-SAY ees-TAH LEEN-doo kom EH-sa HOE-pa (to a man).*

**You look beautiful.**
Você tá linda. (to a woman) | Você tá lindo. (to a man)
*voe-SAY tah LEEN-da (to a woman) | voe-SAY tah LEEN-doo (to a man)*

**Let me help you out of the car.**
Deixa eu te ajudar a sair do carro.
*DAY-sha AY-oo chee ah-zhoo-DAR ah sah-EEH doo KAH-hoo.*

**Sarah, will you come with me to dinner?**
Sarah, quer vir jantar comigo?
*SAH-rah, kehr veeh zhan-TAH ko-MEE-goo?*

**I would like to ask you out on a date.**
Quero te chamar pra um encontro.
*KEH-roo chee sha-MAH prah oom ayn-KON-tro.*

**Are you free tonight?**
Você tá livre hoje à noite?
*voe-SAY tah LEE-vree OE-zhee ah NOY-chee?*

**This is my phone number. Call me anytime.**
Esse é o meu telefone. Me liga em qualquer horário.
*AY-sy eh oo MAY-oo tay-lay-FOE-nee. Muh LEE-gah ayn kwaw-KEHR oe-RAH-ryo.*

**Can I hug you?**
Posso te dar um abraço?
*POH-soo chee dah oom ah-BRAH-soo?*

**Would you like to sing karaoke?**
Quer ir cantar em um karaoke?
*kehr eer kan-TAH ayn oom ka-ra-oe-KAY?*

**What kind of song would you like to sing?**
Que tipo de música você gosta de cantar?
*kee CHEE-poo gee MOO-zee-ka voe-SAY GOHS-ta gee kan-TAH?*

**Have you ever sung this song before?**
Você já cantou essa música alguma vez?
*voe-SAY zha kan-TOE EH-sa MOO-zee-ka ahw-GOOM-ah vays?*

**We can sing it together.**
Podemos cantar juntos.
*po-DAY-moos kan-TAH ZHOON-toos.*

**Can I kiss you?**
Posso te dar um beijo?
*POH-soo chee dah oom BAY-zhoo?*

**Are you cold?**
Você tá com frio?
*voe-SAY tah kom FREE-oo?*

**We can stay out as late as you want.**
Podemos ficar até quando você quiser.
*po-DAY-moos fee-KAR ah-TEH KWAN-doo voe-SAY kee-ZEH.*

**Please, dinner is on me.**
Por favor, o jantar fica por minha conta.
*poer fa-VOER, oo zhan-TAH FEE-ka poeh MEE-nya KON-ta.*

**Shall we split the bill?**
Vamos dividir a conta?
*VAM-moos gee-vee-GEEH ah KON-ta?*

**We should spend more time together.**
A gente deveria passar mais tempo juntos.
*ah ZHAIN-chee day-vay-RI-a pah-SAR MAH-ees TAYM-poo ZHOON-toos.*

**We should walk the town tonight.**
Vamos dar uma volta pela cidade hoje à noite?
*VAM-moos dah OO-ma VOH-oo-ta PAY-la see-DAH-gee OE-zhee ah NOY-chee.*

**Did you enjoy everything?**
Gostou de tudo?
*goes-TOE gee TOO-doo?*

# MONEY AND SHOPPING

**May I try this on?**
Posso provar?
*POH-soo proe-VAH?*

**How much does this cost?**
Quanto custa?
*KWAN-too KOOS-ta?*

**Do I sign here or here?**
Assino aqui ou aqui?
*ah-SEE-noo ah-KEE oe ah-KEE?*

**Is that your final price?**
Esse é o preço final?
*AY-sy eh oo PRAY-soo fy-NAW?*

**Where do I find toiletries?**
Onde eu acho produtos de higiene pessoal?
*OWN-gee AY-oo AH-shoo proe-DOO-toos gee ee-zhee-AY-nee pay-soe-AH-oo?*

**Would you be willing to take five dollars for this item?**
Podemos deixar por cinco dólares?
*po-DAY-moos day-SHAR poeh SEEN-ko DOH-la-rys?*

**I can't afford it at that price.**
Não tenho como pagar esse valor.
*NANN-oo TAYN-gnoo KOE-moo pa-GAH AY-sy vah-LOEH.*

**I can find this cheaper somewhere else.**
Posso encontrar mais barato em outro lugar.
*POH-soo ayn-kon-TRAH MAH-ees ba-RAH-too ayn OE-troo loo-GAR.*

**Is there a way we can haggle on price?**
Tem como negociar esse preço?
*tayn KOE-moo nay-goe-see-AH AY-sy PRAY-soo?*

**How many of these have sold today?**
Quantos você vendeu hoje?
*KWAN-toos voe-SAY VAIN-dew OE-zhee?*

**Can you wrap that up as a gift?**
Pode embalar para presente?
*POH-gee ayn-ba-LAH PAH-ra pray-ZAYN-chee?*

**Do you provide personalized letters?**
Vocês também têm cartões personalizados?
*voe-SAYS tam-BAYN tayn kah-TOYNS pays-soe-na-lee-ZAH-doos?*

**I would like this to be specially delivered to my hotel.**
Eu queria que entregassem no meu hotel.
*AY-oo kay-REE-ah kee ayn-tray-GAH-sayn noo MAY-oo oe-TEHW.*

**Can you help me, please?**
Pode me ajudar, por favor?
*POH-gee mee ah-zhoo-DAR, poer fa-VOER?*

**We should go shopping at the market.**
Precisamos ir fazer compras no mercado.
*pray-see-ZAM-moos eer fah-ZAYR KOM-pras noo mayh-KA-doo.*

**Are you keeping track of the clothes that fit me?**
Você tá lembrando das roupas que cabem em mim?
*voe-SAY tah layn-BRAN-doo das HOE-pas kee KA-bayn ayn meen?*

**Can I have one size up?**
Você tem um tamanho maior?
*voe-SAY tayn oom tam-MAN-gnoo mah-ee-OHR?*

**How many bathrooms does the apartment have?**
Quantos banheiros tem no apartamento?
*KWAN-toos bahn-GNAY-roos tayn noo ah-par-ta-MAYN-too?*

**Where's the kitchen?**
Onde é a cozinha?
*OWN-gee eh ah koe-ZEEN-nya?*

**Does this apartment have a gas or electric stove?**
Esse apartamento tem gás ou fogão elétrico?
*AY-sy ah-par-ta-MAYN-too tayn GAH-ees oe foe-GAWM ay-LEH-tree-koo?*

**Is there a spacious backyard?**
Tem quintal grande?
*tayn keen-TAHW GRAN-gee?*

**How much is the down payment?**
Quanto é a entrada?
*KWAN-too eh ah ayn-TRA-da?*

**I'm looking for a furnished apartment.**
Estou procurando um apartamento mobiliado.
ees-TOE pro-koo-RAN-doo oom *ah-par-ta-MAYN-too moh-bee-LEEAH-doh*

**I need a two-bedroom apartment to rent.**
Preciso de um apartamento de dois quartos pra alugar.
*pray-SEE-zoo gee oom ah-par-ta-MAYN-too gee doys KWAR-toos prah ah-loo-GAR.*

**I'm looking for an apartment with utilities paid.**
Estou procurando um apartamento com todas as despesas inclusas.
*ees-TOE pro-koo-RAN-doo oom ah-par-ta-MAYN-too kom TOE-das ahs gees-PAY-zas een-KLOO-zas.*

**The carpet in this apartment needs to be pulled up.**
O tapete desse apartamento precisa ser removido.
*oo tah-PAY-chee DAY-sy ah-par-ta-MAYN-too prAY-sy-za sayh hay-moe-VEE-doo.*

**I need you to come down on the price of this apartment.**
Tem como baixar um pouco mais esse preço?
*tayn KOE-moo bye-SHAR oom POE-koo MAH-ees AY-sy PRAY-soo?*

**Will I be sharing this place with other people?**
Vou dividir o local com mais alguém?
*voe gee-vee-GEEH oo loe-KAW kom MAH-ees AHW-gain?*

**How do you work the fireplace?**
Como funciona a lareira?
*KOE-moo foon-see-OE-na ah lah-RAY-ra?*

**Are there any curfew rules attached to this apartment?**
Tem alguma regra com alguma restrição para o horário da noite?
*tayn ahw-GOOM-ah HEH-gra kom ahw-GOOM-ah hays-tree-SAWM PAH-ra oo oe-RAH-ryo dah NOY-chee?*

**How long is the lease for this place?**
Por quantos dias esse espaço vai estar disponível para ser alugado?
*poeh KWAN-toos GEE-ahs AY-sy ees-PAH-soo VAH-ee ees-TAH gees-poe-NEE-vew PAH-ra sayh ah-loo-GAH-doo?*

**Do you gamble?**
Você gosta de jogos de apostas?
*voe-SAY GOHS-ta gee ZHOH-goos gee ah-POHS-tas?*

**We should go to a casino.**
A gente deveria ir em um cassino.
*ah ZHAIN-chee day-vay-RI-a eer ayn oom kah-SEE-noo.*

**There is really good horse racing in this area.**
Tem uma corrida de cavalos muito boa por aqui.
*tayn OO-ma koe-HEE-da gee ka-VAH-loos MOON-ee-too BOE-ah poer ah-KEE.*

**Do you have your ID so that we can go gambling?**
Você está com a sua identidade, para irmos jogar?
*voe-SAY ees-TAH kom ah SOO-a ee-dayn-chee-DAH-gee, PAH-ra EER-moos zhoe-GAR?*

**Who did you bet on?**
Você apostou em quem?
*Voe-SAY ah-poes-TOE ayn kayn?*

**I am calling about the apartment that you placed in the ad.**
Estou ligando sobre o apartamento que você anunciou.
*ees-TOE lee-GAN-doo SOE-bree oo ah-par-ta-MAYN-too kee voe-SAY ah-noon-see-OE.*

**How much did you bet?**
Quanto você apostou?
*KWAN-too voe-SAY ah-poes-TOE?*

**We should go running with the bulls!**
Vamos para a corrida de touros!
*VAM-moos PAH-ra ah koe-HEE-da gee TOE-roos!*

**Is Adele coming to sing at this venue tonight?**
Adele vai cantar nesse local hoje?
*ah-DEH-lee VAH-ee kan-TAH NAY-sy loe-KAW OE-zhee?*

**How much is the item you have by the window?**
Quanto custa esse item que você tem na vitrine?
*KWAN-too KOOS-ta AY-sy EE-tayn kee voe-SAY tayn nah vee-TREE-nee?*

**Do you have payment plans?**
Vocês parcelam?
*voe-SAYS pah-SEH-lawm?*

**Do these two items come together?**
Esses dois itens vêm juntos?
*AY-sees doys EE-tayns vayn ZHOON-toos?*

**Are these parts cheaply made?**
Essas peças são mais baratas?
*EH-sas PEH-sas sawm MAH-y bah-RAH-tas?*

**This is a huge bargain!**
O preço está muito bom!
*oo PRAY-soo ees-TAH MOON-ee-too bown!*

**I like this. How does three hundred dollars sound?**
Gostei dessa peça. Podemos fechar por trezentos dólares?
*goes-TAY DEH-sa PEH-sa. po-DAY-moos fay-SHAR poeh tray-ZAYN-toos DOH-la-rys?*

**Two hundred is all I can offer. That is my final price.**
Duzentos é o que eu posso pagar. É o meu preço final.
*doo-ZAIN-toos eh oo kee AY-oo POH-soo pah-GAH. eh oo MAY-oo PRAY-soo fy-NAW.*

**Do you have cheaper versions of this item?**
Você tem alguma peça mais barata?
*voe-SAY tayn ahw-GOOM-ah PEH-sa MAH-ees bah-RAH-ta?*

**Do you have the same item with a different pattern?**
Você tem outro modelo dessa mesma peça?
*voe-SAY tayn OE-troo moe-DAY-loo DEH-sa MAYZ-ma PEH-sa?*

**How much is this worth?**
Qual é o valor?
*kwaw eh oo vah-LOEH?*

**Can you pack this up and send it to my address that's on file?**
Você pode empacotar e levar para o endereço que está na ficha?
*voe-SAY POH-gee ayn-pa-koe-TAH y lay-VAH PAH-ra oo ayn-day-RAY-soo kee ees-TAH nah FEE-sha?*

**Does it fit?**
Cabe?
KAH-bee?

**They are too big for me.**
Está muito grande em mim.
*ees-TAH MOON-ee-too GRAN-gee ayn meen.*

**Please find me another but in the same size.**
Por favor, procure outra peça no mesmo tamanho.
*poer fa-VOER, proe-KOO-ree OE-tra PEH-sa noo MAYZ-moo ta-MAN-gnoo.*

**It fits, but is tight around my waist.**
Cabe, mas fica apertado na minha cintura.
*KAH-bee, MAH-ees FEE-ka ah-PAYH-tah-doo nah MEE-nya seen-TOO-ra.*

**Can I have one size down?**
Posso ver um tamanho menor?
*POH-soo vayh oom ta-MAN-gnoo may-NOR?*

**Size twenty, American.**
Tamanho vinte, pelo padrão americano.
*ta-MAN-gnoo VEEN-chee, PAY-loo pah-DRAWM ah-may-ree-KAN-noo.*

**Do you sell appliances for the home?**
Você vende eletrodomésticos?
*voe-SAY VAYN-gee ay-leh-troe-doe-MEHS-chee-koos?*

**Not now, thank you.**
Agora não, obrigado.
*ah-GOH-ra NANN-oo, oe-bree-GAH-doo.*

**I'm looking for something special.**
Estou procurando algo especial.
*ees-TOE pro-koo-RAN-doo AHW-goo ays-pay-see-AH-oo.*

**I'll call you when I need you.**
Quando eu precisar, eu te ligo.
*KWAN-doo AY-oo pray-see-ZAR, AY-oo chee LEE-goo.*

**Do you have this in my size?**
Você tem essa peça no meu tamanho?
*voe-SAY tayn EH-sa PEH-sa noo MAY-oo ta-MAN-gnoo?*

**On which floor can I find cologne?**
Onde fica a seção de perfumes?
*OWN-gee FEE-ka ah say-SAWM gee payh-FOO-mees?*

**Where is the entrance?**
Onde é a entrada?
*OWN-gee eh ah ayn-TRA-da?*

**Do I exit from that door?**
Saio por essa porta?
*SAH-yo poer EH-sa POHR-ta?*

**Where is the elevator?**
Onde é o elevador?
*OWN-gee eh oo ay-lay-vah-DOEH?*

**Do I push or pull to get this door open?**
Empurro ou puxo para abrir essa porta?
*ayn-POO-hoo ow POO-shoo PAH-ra ah-BREEH EH-sa POHR-ta?*

**I already have that, thanks.**
Já tenho, obrigado.
*zha TAYN-gnoo, oe-bree-GAH-doo.*

**Where can I try this on?**
Onde posso provar?
*OWN-gee POH-soo proe-VAH?*

**This mattress is very soft.**
Esse colchão é muito macio.
*AY-sy koe-SHWAM eh MOON-ee-too mah-SEE-oo.*

**What is a good place for birthday gifts?**
Você conhece algum lugar para comprar presente de aniversário?
*Voe-SAY koe-GNEH-see ahw-GOOM loo-GAR PAH-ra kom-PRAH pray-ZAYN-chee gee ah-nee-vayh-SAH-ryu?*

**I'm just looking, but thank you.**
Estou só olhando, obrigado.
*ees-TOEsoh OE-lyan-doo, oe-bree-GAH-doo.*

**Yes, I will call you when I need you, thank you.**
Sim, quando precisar eu te ligo, obrigado.
*seem, KWAN-doo pray-see-ZAR AY-oo chee LEE-goo, oe-bree-GAH-doo.*

**Do you accept returns?**
Se precisar, eu posso trocar?
*see pray-see-ZAR, AY-oo POH-soo troe-KAH?*

**Here is my card and receipt for the return.**
Aqui está o meu cartão e a nota para a devolução.
*ah-KEE ees-TAH oo MAY-oo kah-TAWM y ah NOH-ta PAH-ra ah day-voe-loo-SAWM.*

**Where are the ladies' clothes?**
Onde ficam as roupas femininas?
*OWN-gee FEE-kam ahs HOE-pas fay-mee-NEE-nas?*

**What sizes are available for this item?**
Quais tamanhos você tem?
*KWA-ees tah-MAN-gnoos voe-SAYS tayn?*

**Is there an ATM machine nearby?**
Tem algum caixa eletrônico por aqui?
*tayn ahw-GOOM KAH-ee-sha ay-lay-TROE-nee-koo poer ah-KEE?*

**What forms of payment do you accept?**
Quais formas de pagamento vocês aceitam?
*KWA-ees FOH-mas gee pah-gah-MAIN-to voe-SAYS ah-SAY-tam?*

**That doesn't interest me.**
Não tenho interesse.
*NANN-oo TAYN-gnoo een-tay-RAY-sy.*

**I don't like it, but thank you.**
Não gosto, mas obrigado.
*NANN-oo GOSH-too, MAH-ees oe-bree-GAH-doo.*

**Do you take American dollars?**
Vocês aceitam dólares?
*voe-SAYS ah-SAY-tam DOH-la-rys?*

**Can you make changes for me?**
Vocês trocam, por favor?
*voe-SAYS TROH-kam, poer fa-VOER?*

**What is the closest place to get change for my money?**

Qual é o lugar mais próximo para trocar dinheiro?

*kwaw eh oo loo-GAR MAH-ees PROH-see-moo PAH-ra troe-KAH dee-GNAY-roo?*

**Are travelers checks able to be changed here?**

Vocês trocam cheques de viagem aqui?

*voe-SAYS TROH-kam SHEH-kees gee vy-AH-zhayn ah-KEE?*

**What is the current exchange rate?**

Quais são as taxas de câmbio atuais?

*KWA-ees sawm ahs TAH-shas gee KAM-byo ah-too-AH-ees?*

**What is the closest place to exchange money?**

Qual é a casa de câmbio mais próxima?

*kwaw eh ah KAH-za gee KAM-byu MAH-ees PROH-see-ma?*

**Do you need to borrow money? How much?**

Você quer dinheiro emprestado? Quanto?

*voe-SAY kehr dee-GNAY-roo ayn-prays-TAH-doo? KWAN-too?*

**Can this bank exchange my money?**

Posso fazer câmbio nesse banco?

*POH-soo fah-ZAYR KAM-byo NAY-sy BAN-koo?*

**What is the exchange rate for the American dollar?**

Qual é a taxa de câmbio para dólar americano?

*kwaw eh ah TAH-sha gee KAM-byo PAH-ra DOH-lah ah-may-ree-KAN-noo?*

**Will you please exchange me fifty dollars?**

Troca pra mim cinquenta dólares, por favor?

*TROH-ka prah meen seen-KWEN-ta DOH-la-rys, poer fa-VOER?*

**I would like a receipt for that.**

Me dê um recibo, por favor.

*mee day oom hay-SEE-boo, poer fa-VOER.*

**Your commission rate is too high.**

Essa taxa de comissão está muito alta.

*EH-sa TAH-sha gee koe-mee-SAWM ees-TAH MOON-ee-too AHW-ta.*

**Does this bank have a lower commission rate?**
Esse banco tem uma taxa de comissão menor?
*AY-sy BAN-koo tayn OO-ma TAH-sha gee koe-mee-SAWM may-NOR?*

**Do you take cash?**
Vocês aceitam dinheiro em espécie?
*voe-SAYS ah-SAY-tam dee-GNAY-roo ayn ays-PEH-sye?*

**Where can I exchange dollars?**
Onde posso trocar dólares?
*OWN-gee POH-soo troe-KAH DOH-la-rys?*

**I want to exchange dollars for yen.**
Quero trocar dólares por ienes.
*KEH-roo troe-KAH DOH-la-rys poeh YEN-es.*

**Do you take credit cards?**
Vocês aceitam cartão de crédito?
*voe-SAYS ah-SAY-tam kah-TAWM gee KREH-gee-too?*

**Here is my credit card.**
Aqui está o meu cartão de crédito.
*ah-KEE ees-TAH oo MAY-oo incklkah-TAWM gee KREH-gee-too.*

**One moment, let me check the receipt.**
Um momento, deixe eu conferir o recibo.
*oom moe-MAIN-too, DAY-shee AY-oo kon-fay-REEH oo hay-SEE-boo.*

**Do I need to pay tax?**
Preciso pagar alguma taxa?
*pray-SEE-zoo pa-GAH ahw-GOOM-ah TAH-sha?*

**How much is this item with tax?**
Quanto custa, já com as taxas inclusas?
*KWAN-too KOOS-ta, zha kom ahs TAH-shas een-KLOO-zas?*

**Where is the cashier?**
Onde é o caixa?
*OWN-gee eh oo KAH-ee-sha?*

**Excuse me, I'm looking for a dress.**
Com licença, estou procurando um vestido.
*KOM lee-SAIN-sa, ees-TOE pro-koo-RAN-doo oom vays-CHEE-doo.*

**That's a lot for that dress.**
O preço do vestido está muito alto.
*oo PRAY-soo doo vays-CHEE-doo ees-TAH MOON-ee-too AHW-too.*

**Sorry, but I don't want it.**
Desculpa, mas não quero.
*gees-KOO-pa, MAH-ees NANN-oo KEH-roo.*

**Okay I will take it.**
Okay, vou levar.
*Oh-KAY, voe lay-VAH.*

**I'm not interested if you are going to sell it at that price.**
Se for esse preço, eu não tenho interesse.
*see foeh AY-sy PRAY-soo, AY-oo NANN-oo TAYN-gnoo een-tay-RAY-sy.*

**You are cheating me at the current price.**
Com esse preço, você está querendo me enganar.
*kom AY-sy PRAY-soo, voe-SAY ees-TAH kay-RAIN-doo mee ayn-gan-NAH.*

**No thanks. I'll only take it if you lower the price by half.**
Não, obrigado. Só levo se o preço cair pela metade.
*nawm, oe-bree-GAH-doo. soh LEH-voo see oo PRAY-soo ka-EER PAY-la may-TAH-gee.*

**That is a good price, I'll take it.**
É um bom preço, eu aceito.
*eh oom bowm PRAY-soo, AY-oo ah-SAY-too.*

**Do you sell souvenirs for tourists?**
Você vende lembranças para turistas?
*voe-SAY VAYN-gee layn-BRAN-sas PAH-ra too-REES-tas?*

**Can I have a bag for that?**
Você pode me dar uma sacola?
*voe-SAY POH-gee mee dah OO-ma sah-KOH-la?*

**Is this the best bookstore in the city?**
Essa é a melhor livraria da cidade?
*EH-sa eh ah may-LYOR lee-vra-REE-ah da see-DAH-gee?*

**I would like to go to a game shop to buy comic books.**
Eu queria ir a uma loja de jogos para comprar quadrinhos.

*AY-oo kay-REE-ah eeh ah OO-ma LOH-zha gee ZHOH-goos PAH-ra kom-PRAH kwa-DREE-gnoos.*

## Are you able to ship my products overseas?

Você consegue enviar o meu produto para outro país?

*Voe-SAY koen-SEH-ghee ayn-vee-AR oo MAY-oo proe-DOO-too PAH-ra OE-troo pah-EES?*

# CHILDREN AND PETS

**Which classroom does my child attend?**

Qual sala de aula é a do meu filho? (for a boy) | Qual sala de aula é a da minha filha? (for a girl)

*kwaw SAH-la gee AHW-la eh ah doo MAY-oo FEE-lyo? (for a boy) | kwaw SAH-la gee AHW-la eh dah dah MEE-nya FEE-lya? (for a girl)*

**Is the report due before the weekend?**

O boletim fica pronto antes do final de semana?

*oo boe-lay-CHEEN FEE-ka PRON-too AHN-chees doo fy-NAW gee say-MANN-na?*

**I'm waiting for my mom to pick me up.**

Estou esperando a minha mãe me buscar.

*ees-TOE ays-pay-RAN-doo ah MEE-nya MANN-ee mee boos-KAH.*

**What time does the school bus run?**

Que horas vai chegar o ônibus escolar?

*kee OH-ras VAH-ee shay-GAH oo OWN-nee-boos ees-koh-LAH?*

**I need to see the principal.**

Preciso falar com o diretor.

*pray-SEE-zoo fah-LAR kom oo gee-ray-TOEH.*

**I would like to report bullying.**

Quero denunciar um caso de bullying.

*KEH-roo day-noon-see-AH oom KAH-zoo gee BOO-lee-een.*

**What are the leash laws in this area?**

Aqui tem alguma lei em relação a cachorro?

*ah-KEE tayn ahw-GOOM-ah lay ayn hay-la-SAWM ah ka-SHOW-hoo?*

**Please keep your dog away from mine.**

Por favor, deixe o seu cachorro longe do meu.

*poer fa-VOER, DAY-shee oo SAY-oo ka-SHOW-hoo LON-gee doo MAY-oo.*

**My dog doesn't bite.**
O meu cachorro não morde.
*oo MAY-oo ka-SHOW-hoo NANN-oo MOHR-gee.*

**I am allergic to cat hair.**
Tenho alergia a pelo de gato.
*TAYN-gnoo ah-layr-GEE-ahh PAY-loo gee GAH-too.*

**Don't leave the door open or the cat will run out!**
Não deixe a porta aberta porque o gato pode sair!
*NANN-oo DAY-shee ah POHR-ta ah-BEHR-ta poor-KAY oo GAH-too POH-gee sah-EEH!*

**Have you fed the dog yet?**
Você já deu comida para o cachorro?
*voe-SAY zha DAY-oo koe-MEE-da PAH-ra oo ka-SHOW-hoo?*

**We need to take the dog to the veterinarian.**
Precisamos levar o cachorro para o veterinário.
*pray-see-ZAM-moos lay-VAH oo ka-SHOW-hoo PAH-ra oo vay-tay-ree-NAH-ree-oo.*

**Are there any open roster spots on the team?**
Tem vaga no time?
*tayn VAH-ga noo CHEE-me?*

**My dog is depressed.**
O cachorro está com depressão.
*oo MAY-oo ka-SHOW-hoo ees-TAH kom day-pray-SAWM.*

**Don't feed the dog table scraps.**
Não alimente o cachorro com restos de comida.
*NANN-oo ah-lee-MAYN-chee oo ka-SHOW-hoo kom HEHS-toos gee koe-MEE-da.*

**Don't let the cat climb up on the furniture.**
Não deixe o gato subir nos móveis.
*NANN-oo DAY-shee oo GAH-too soo-BEEH noos MOH-vays.*

**The dog is not allowed to sleep in the bed with you.**
O cachorro não pode dormir na cama com você.
*oo ka-SHOE-hoo NANN-oo POH-gee doeh-MEEH na KA-ma kom voe-SAY.*

**There is dog poop on the floor. Clean it up.**
Tem cocô de cachorro no chão. Limpa, por favor.
*tayn koe-KOE gee ka-SHOE-hoo noo shawm. LEEM-pa, poer fa-VOER.*

**When was the last time you took the dog for a walk?**
Quando foi a última vez que você levou o cachorro pra passear?
*KWAN-doo foy ah OO-chee-ma vays kee voe-SAY lay-VOE oo ka-SHOW-hoo prah pah-say-AH?*

**Are you an international student? How long are you attending?**
Você é intercambista? Vai ficar aqui por quanto tempo?
*voe-SAY eh een-tayh-kam-BEES-ta? VAH-ee fee-KAR ah-KEE KWAN-too TAYM-poo?*

**Are you a French student?**
Você estuda francês?
*voe-SAY ays-TOO-da fran-SAYS?*

**I am an American student that is here for the semester.**
Sou americano e estou aqui nesse semestre para estudar.
*soe ah-may-ree-KAN-noo y ees-TOE ah-KEE NAY-sy say-MEHS-tree PAH-ra ays-too-DAH.*

**Please memorize this information.**
Decore essa informação, por favor.
*day-KOH-ree EH-sa een-foeh-mah-SAWM, poer fa-VOER.*

**This is my roommate Max.**
Esse é o Max, meu colega de quarto.
*AY-sy eh oo Max, MAY-oo koe-LEH-ga gee KWAR-too.*

**Are these questions likely to appear on the exams?**
Essas questões podem aparecer na prova?
*EH-sas kays-TOYNS POH-dayn ah-pah-RHE-say nah PROH-va?*

**Teacher, say that once more, please.**
Male: Professor, o senhor pode repetir?
*proe-fay-SOER, oo-saign-OH POH-gee hay-pay-CHEER?*
Female: Professora, a senhora pode repetir?
*proe-fay-SOE-ra, ah sain-GNOH-ra POH-gee hay-pay-CHEER?*

**I didn't do well on the quiz.**
Não fui bem no teste.
*NANN-oo fooy bayn noo TEHS-chee.*

**Go play outside, but stay where I can see you.**
Vá brincar lá fora, mas fique onde eu possa te ver.
*vah breen-KAH lah FOH-ra, MAH-ees FEE-ky OWN-gee AY-oo POH-sa chee vayh.*

**How is your daughter?**
Como está a sua filha?
*KOE-moo ees-TAH ah SOO-a FEE-lya?*

**I'm going to walk the dog.**
Vou passear com o cachorro.
*voe pah-say-AH kom oo ka-SHOE-hoo.*

**She's not very happy here.**
Ela não está muito feliz aqui.
*EH-la NANN-oo ees-TAH MOON-ee-too fay-LEES ah-KEE.*

**I passed the quiz with high marks!**
Passei na prova com boas notas!
*pah-SAY nah PROH-va kom BOE-as NOH-tas!*

**What program are you enrolled in?**
Em que programa você está matriculado?
*ayn kee proe-GRAM-ma voe-SAY ees-TAH mah-tree-koo-LAH-doo?*

**I really like my English teacher.**
Gosto muito do meu professor de inglês.
*GOSH-too MOON-ee-too doo MAY-oo proe-fay-SOER gee een-GLAYS.*

**I have too much homework to do.**
Tenho muito dever de casa pra fazer.
*TAYN-gnoo MOON-ee-too day-VAYH gee KAH-za prah fah-ZAYR.*

**Tomorrow, I have to take my dog to the vet.**
Amanhã tenho que levar o meu cachorro pro veterinário.
*ah-man-GNAN TAYN-gnoo kee lay-VAH oo MAY-oo ka-SHOW-hoo proo vay-tay-ree-NAH-ree-oo.*

**When do we get to go to lunch?**
Quando vamos almoçar?
*KWAN-doo VAM-moos ah-oo-moe-SAH?*

**My dog swallowed something he shouldn't have.**
O meu cachorro engoliu alguma coisa que não deveria.
*oo MAY-oo ka-SHOE-hoo ayn-goe-LYU ahw-GOOM-ah KOY-za kee NANN-oo day-vay-RI-a.*

**We need more toys for our dogs to play with.**
Precisamos de mais brinquedos para os nossos cachorros brincarem.
*pray-see-ZAM-moos gee MAH-ees breen-KAY-doos PAH-ra oos NOH-soos ka-SHOE-hoos breen-KA-rayn.*

**Can you please change the litter box?**
Você pode trocar a caixa de areia?
*voe-SAY POH-gee troe-KAH ah KAH-ee-sha gee ah-RAY-ah?*

**Get a lint brush and roll it to get the hair off your clothes.**
Pegue uma escova pra tirar o pelo das suas roupas.
*PEH-ghee OO-ma ays-KOE-va prah chee-RAH oo PAY-loo das SOO-as HOE-pas.*

**Can you help me study?**
Você pode me ajudar a estudar?
*voe-SAY POH-gee mee ah-zhoo-DAR ah ays-too-DAH?*

**I have to go study in my room.**
Tenho que ir estudar no meu quarto.
*TAYN-gnoo kee eer ays-too-DAH noo MAY-oo KWAR-too.*

**We went to the campus party, and it was a lot of fun.**
Fomos a uma festa da universidade, foi super divertido.
*FOE-moos ah OO-ma FEHS-tah dah oo-nee-vayh-see-DAH-gee, foy SOO-peh gee-vayh-CHEE-doo.*

**Can you use that word in a sentence?**
Você consegue formar uma frase com essa palavra?
*Voe-SAY kon-SEH-ghee foeh-MAH OO-ma FRAH-zee kom EH-sa pah-LAH-vra?*

**How do you spell that word?**
Como se soletra essa palavra?
*KOE-moo see soe-LEH-tra EH-sa pah-LAH-vra?*

**Go play with your brother.**
Vá brincar com o seu irmão.
*vah breen-KAH kom oo SAY-oo eer-MAWM.*

**Come inside! It is dinnertime.**
Entra! É hora do jantar.
*AYN-tra! eh OH-ra doo zhan-TAH.*

**Tell me about your day.**
Me conta como foi o seu dia.
*mee KON-ta KOE-moo foy oo SAY-oo GEE-ah.*

**Is there anywhere you want to go?**
Você quer ir pra algum lugar?
*voe-SAY kehr eer prah ahw-GOOM loo-GAR?*

**How are you feeling?**
Como você está se sentindo?
*KOE-moo voe-SAY ees-TAH see sayn-CHEEN-doo?*

**What do you want me to make for dinner tonight?**
O que você quer que eu faça pra jantar hoje?
*oo kee voe-SAY kehr kee AY-oo FAH-sa prah zhan-TAH OE-zhee?*

**It's time for you to take a bath.**
É hora de ir tomar banho.
*eh OH-ra gee eer toe-MAH BAN-gnoo.*

**Brush your teeth and wash behind your ears.**
Escove os dentes e lave atrás das orelhas.
*ays-KOH-vee oos DAYN-chees ee LAH-vee ah-TRAH-ys das oe-RAY-lyas.*

**You're not wearing that to bed.**
Você não veste isso pra dormir.
*voe-SAY NANN-oo VEHS-chee EE-soo prah doeh-MEEH.*

**I don't like the way you're dressed. Put something else on.**
Não gostei dessa roupa que você colocou. Veste outra coisa.
*NANN-oo GOES-tay DEH-sa HOE-pa kee voe-SAY koe-loe-KOE. VEHS-chee OE-tra KOY-za.*

**Did you make any friends today?**
Você fez amigos novos hoje?
*Voe-SAY fays ah-MEE-goos NOH-voos OE-zhee?*

**Let me see your homework.**
Deixa eu ver o seu dever de casa.
*DAY-sha AY-oo vayh oo SAY-oo day-VEH gee KAH-za.*

**Do I need to call your school?**
Preciso ligar pra sua escola?
*pray-SEE-zoo lee-GAR prah SOO-a ees-KOH-la?*

**The dog can't go outside right now.**
O cachorro não pode sair agora.
*oo ka-SHOE-hoo NANN-oo POH-gee sah-EEH ah-GOH-ra.*

**Is the new quiz going to be available next week?**
O novo teste vai estar disponível na semana que vem?
*oo NOE-voo TEHS-chee VAH-ee ees-TAH gees-poe-NEE-vew nah say-MANN-na kee vayn?*

**Are we allowed to use calculators with the test?**
Pode usar calculadora durante a prova?
*POH-gee oo-ZAR kah-oo-koo-lah-DOE-ra doo-RANN-chee ah PROH-va?*

**I would like to lead today's lesson.**
Eu queria conduzir a aula de hoje.
*AY-oo kay-REE-ah kon-doo-ZEEH ah AHW-la gee OE-zhee.*

**I have a dorm curfew, so I need to go back.**
Tenho que chegar no dormitório na hora certa, por isso preciso voltar.
*TAYN-gnoo kee shay-GAH noo doeh-mee-TOH-ree-oo nah OH-ra SEH-ta, poer EE-soo pray-SEE-zoo voe-TAH.*

**Do I have to use pencil or ink?**
Tenho que usar lápis ou caneta?
*TAYN-gnoo kee oo-ZAR LAH-pees oe kah-NAY-ta?*

**Are cell phones allowed in class?**
É permitido usar celular na sala de aula?
*eh payr-mee-CHEE-doo oo-ZAR say-LOO-lah nah SAH-la gee AHW-la?*

**Where can I find the nearest dog park?**
Onde fica o parque de cachorros mais próximo?
*OWN-gee FEE-ka oo PAHR-kee gee ka-SHOW-hoos MAH-ees PROH-see-moo?*

**Are dogs allowed to be off their leash here?**
Os cachorros podem ficar sem coleira aqui?
*oos ka-SHOW-hoos POH-dayn fee-KAR sayn koe-LAY-ra ah-KEE?*

**Are children allowed here?**
Permitem crianças aqui?
*payr-MEE-tayn kry-AN-sas ah-KEE?*

**I would like to set up a play date with our children.**
Eu queria marcar um dia para os nossos filhos brincarem.
*AY-oo kay-REE-ah mar-KAR oom GEE-ahh PAH-rah oos NOH-soos FEE-lyos breen-KA-rayn.*

**I would like to invite you to my child's birthday party.**
Quero te convidar pra festa de aniversário do meu filho.
*KEH-roo chee kon-vee-DAH prah FEHS-tah gee ah-nee-vayh-SAH-ryu doo MAY-oo FEE-lyo.*

**Did you miss your dorm curfew last night?**
Você perdeu a hora de ir dormir no seu dormitório ontem?
*voe-SAY payh-DAY-oo ah OH-ra gee eer doeh-MEEH noo SAY-oo doeh-mee-TOH-ree-oo OWN-tayn?*

# TRAVELER'S GUIDE

**Over there is the library.**
Ali é a biblioteca.
*ah-LEE eh ah bee-blee-oe-TEH-ka.*

**Just over there.**
Bem ali.
*bayn ah-LEE.*

**Yes, this way.**
Sim, por aqui.
*seem*, poer *ah-KEE.*

**I haven't done anything wrong.**
Não fiz nada de errado.
*NANN-oo fees NAH-da gee ay-HA-doo.*

**It was a misunderstanding.**
Foi um mal entendido.
*foy oom MAH-oo ayn-tayn-GEE-doo.*

**I am an American citizen.**
Sou cidadão americano.
*soe si-da-DAWM ah-may-ree-KAN-noo.*

**We are tourists on vacation.**
Somos turistas de férias.
*SOE-moos too-REES-tas gee FEH-ree-as.*

**I am looking for an apartment.**
Estou procurando um apartamento.
*ees-TOE pro-koo-RAN-doo oom ah-par-ta-MAYN-too.*

**This is a short-term stay.**
É por pouco tempo.
*eh poeh POE-koo TAYM-poo.*

**I am looking for a place to rent.**
Estou procurando um lugar pra alugar.
*ees-TOE pro-koo-RAN-doo oom loo-GAR prah ah-loo-GAR.*

**Where can we grab a quick bite to eat?**
Onde podemos conseguir alguma coisa pra comer?
*OWN-gee po-DAY-moos kon-say-GHEEH ahw-GOOM-ah KOY-za prah koe-MEHR?*

**We need the cheapest place you can find.**
Precisamos do lugar mais barato que você encontrar.
*pray-see-ZAM-moos doo loo-GAR MAH-ees bah-RAH-too kee voe-SAY ayn-kon-TRAH.*

**Do you have a map of the city?**
Você tem um mapa da cidade?
*voe-SAY tayn oom MAH-pa dah see-DAH-gee?*

**What places do tourists usually visit when they come here?**
Quais são as atrações turísticas daqui?
*KWA-ees sawm ahs ah-tra-SOYNS too-REES-chee-kas dah-KEE?*

**Can you take our picture, please?**
Pode tirar uma foto, por favor?
*POH-gee chee-RAH OO-ma FOH-too, poer fa-VOER?*

**Do you take foreign credit cards?**
Vocês aceitam cartões de crédito estrangeiros?
*voe-SAYS ah-SAY-tam kah-TOYNS gee KREH-gee-too ays-tran-ZHAY-roos?*

**I would like to hire a bicycle to take us around the city.**
Eu gostaria de alugar uma bicicleta para dar uma volta.
*EY-oo goes-ta-REE-a gee ah-loo-GAR OO-ma bee-see-KLEH-ta PAH-ra dah OO-ma VOH-oo-ta.*

**Do you mind if I take pictures here?**
Posso tirar fotos aqui?
*POH-soo chee-RAH FOH-toos ah-KEE?*

# ANSWERS

**Yes, to some extent.**
Sim, um pouco.
*seem, oom POE-koo.*

**I'm not sure.**
Não tenho certeza.
*NANN-oo TAYN-gnoo sayr-TAY-za.*

**Yes, go ahead.**
Sim, pode falar.
*seem, POH-gee fah-LAR.*

**Yes, just like you.**
Sim, assim como você.
*seem, ah-SEEM KOE-moo voe-SAY.*

**No, no problem at all.**
Não, não tem problema nenhum.
*NANN-oo, NANN-oo tayn proe-BLAY-mah nain-GNOOM.*

**This is a little more expensive than the other item.**
Esse é um pouco mais caro do que o outro.
*AY-sy eh oom POE-koo MAH-ees KAH-roo doo kee oo OE-troo.*

**My city is small but nice.**
A minha cidade é pequena, mas agradável.
*ah MEE-nya see-DAH-gee eh pay-KEN-na, MAH-ees ah-gra-DAH-vew.*

**This city is quite big.**
Essa cidade é muito grande.
*EH-sa see-DAH-gee eh MOON-ee-too GRAN-gee.*

**I'm from America.**
Sou dos Estados Unidos.
*soe doos ays-TAH-doos oo-NEE-doos.*

**We'll wait for you.**
Vamos esperar você.
*VAM-moos ays-pay-RAH voe-SAY.*

**I love going for walks.**
Adoro fazer caminhada.
*ah-DOH-roo fah-ZAYR ka-mee-GNAH-da.*

**I'm a woman.**
Sou mulher.
*soe moo-LYER.*

**Good, I'm going to see it.**
Tudo bem, eu vou ver isso.
*TOO-doo bayn, AY-oo voe vayh EE-soo.*

**So do I.**
Eu também.
*AY-oo tam-BAYN.*

**I'll think about it and call you tomorrow with an answer.**
Vou pensar sobre isso e te ligar amanhã com uma resposta.
*voe PAIN-sar SOE-bree EE-soo y tee lee-GAR ah-man-GNAN kom OO-ma hays-POHS-ta.*

**I have two children.**
Tenho dois filhos.
*TAYN-gnoo doys FEE-lyos.*

**Does this place have a patio?**
Tem algum terraço?
*tayn ahw-GOOM tay-HAH-soo?*

**No, the bathroom is vacant.**
Não, não tem ninguém no banheiro.
*NANN-oo, NANN-oo tayn neen-GAYN noo bahn-GNAY-roo.*

**I'm not old enough.**
Ainda não tenho idade suficiente.
*ah-EEN-da NANN-oo TAYN-gnoo ee-DAH-gee soo-fee-see-AYN-chee.*

**No, it is very easy.**
Não, é muito fácil.
*NANN-oo, eh MOON-ee-too FAH-seew.*

**Understood.**
Entendi.
*ayn-tayn-GEE.*

**Only if you go first.**
Só se você for primeiro.
*soh see voe-SAY foh pree-MAY-roo.*

**Yes, that is correct.**
Sim, está certo.
*seem, ees-TAH SEH-too.*

**That was the wrong answer.**
Foi a resposta errada.
*foy ah hays-POHS-ta ay-HA-dah.*

**We haven't decided yet.**
Ainda não decidimos.
*ah-EEN-da NANN-oo day-see-GEE-moos.*

**We can try.**
Podemos tentar.
*po-DAY-moos tayn-TAH.*

**I like to read books.**
Gosto de ler livros.
*GOHS-too gee layh LEE-vros.*

**We can go there together.**
Podemos ir lá juntos.
*po-DAY-moos eer lah ZHOON-toos.*

**Yes, I see.**
Sim, sei.
*seem, say.*

**That looks interesting.**
Parece interessante.
*pah-REH-see een-tay-ray-SAN-chee.*

**Me neither.**
Nem eu.
*nayn AY-oo.*

**It was fun.**
Foi divertido.
*foy gee-vayr-CHEE-doo.*

**Me too.**
Eu também.
*AY-oo tam-BAYN.*

**Stay there.**
Fique aí.
*FEE-ky ah-EE.*

**We were worried about you.**
Estávamos preocupados com você.
*ays-TAH-va-moos pray-oe-koo-PAH-doos kom voe-SAY.*

**No, not really.**
Não, na verdade não.
*NANN-oo, nah vayh-DAH-gee NANN-oo.*

**Unbelievable.**
Inacreditável.
*een-nah-kray-gee-TAH-vew.*

**No, I didn't make it in time.**
Não, não cheguei a tempo.
*NANN-oo, NANN-oo shay-GAY ah TAYM-poo.*

**No, you cannot.**
Não, você não pode.
*NANN-oo, voe-SAY NANN-oo POH-gee.*

**Here you go.**
Lá vai.
*lah VAH-ee.*

**It was good.**
Foi bom.
*foy bowm.*

**Ask my wife.**
Pergunte à minha esposa.
*payh-GOON-chee ah MEE-nya ees-POE-za.*

**That's up to him.**
Ele decide.
*AY-ly day-SEE-gee.*

**That is not allowed.**
Não é permitido.
*NANN-oo eh payr-mee-CHEE-doo.*

**You can stay at our place.**
Pode ficar com a gente.
*POH-gee fee-KAR kom ah ZHAIN-chee.*

**Only if you want to.**
Só se você quiser.
*soh see voe-SAY kee-ZEH.*

**It depends on my schedule.**
Depende da minha agenda.
*day-PAIN-gee dah MEE-nya ah-ZHAYN-da.*

**I don't think that's possible.**
Acho que não dá.
*AH-shoo kee NANN-oo dah.*

**You're not bothering me.**
Você não está me incomodando.
*voe-SAY NANN-oo ees-TAH mee een-koe-moe-DAN-doo.*

**The salesman will know.**
O vendedor vai saber.
*oo vayn-dayn-DOER VAH-ee sah-BAYH.*

**I have to work.**
Tenho que trabalhar.
*TAYN-gnoo kee tra-ba-LYAR.*

**I'm late.**
Estou atrasado. (masc.) | Estou atrasada (fem.)
*ees-TOE ah-tra-ZAH-doo (masc.) | ees-TOE ah-tra-ZAH-da (fem.)*

**To pray.**
Rezar.
*hay-ZAH.*

**I'll do my best.**
Vou fazer o possível.
*voe fah-ZAYR oo poe-SEE-vew.*

# DIRECTIONS

**Over here.**
Aqui.
*ah-KEE.*

**Go straight ahead.**
Vá em frente.
*vah ayn FRAYN-chee.*

**Follow the straight line.**
Siga em linha reta.
*SEE-ga ayn LEE-gna HEH-ta.*

**Go halfway around the circle.**
Vá até a metade do círculo.
*vah ah-TEH ah may-TAH-gee doo SEER-koo-loo.*

**It is to the left.**
É para a esquerda.
*eh PAH-ra ah ees-KAYR-da.*

**Where is the party going to be?**
Onde vai ser a festa?
*OWN-gee VAH-ee sayh ah FEHS-tah?*

**Where is the library situated?**
Onde é a biblioteca?
*OWN-gee eh ah bee-blee-oe-TEH-ka?*

**It is to the north.**
É em direção ao norte.
*eh ain gee-ray-SAWM AH-oo NOH-chee.*

**You can find it down the street.**
Está no final da rua.
*ees-TAH noo fee-NAW dah HOO-ah.*

135

**Go into the city to get there.**
Vá para a cidade para chegar lá.
*vah PAH-ra ah see-DAH-gee PAH-ra shay-GAH lah.*

**Where are you now?**
Onde você está agora?
*OWN-gee voe-SAY ees-TAH ah-GOH-ra?*

**There is a fire hydrant right in front of me.**
Tem um hidrante bem na minha frente.
*tayn oom ee-dra-TAN-chee bayn nah MEE-nya FRAYN-chee.*

**Do you know a shortcut?**
Você sabe de algum atalho?
*voe-SAY SAH-bee gee ahw-GOOM ah-TAH-lyo?*

**Where is the freeway?**
Onde está a rodovia?
*OWN-gee ees-TAH ah hoe-doe-VEE-a?*

**Do I need exact change for the toll?**
Preciso de dinheiro trocado para o pedágio?
*pray-SEE-zoo gee dee-GNAY-roo troe-KAH-doo PAH-ra oo pay-DAH-zhee-oo?*

**At the traffic light, turn right.**
No semáforo, vire à direita.
*noo suh-MAH-foe-roo, VEE-ree ah gee-RAY-ta.*

**When you get to the intersection, turn left.**
Quando chegar no cruzamento, vire à esquerda.
*KWAN-doo shay-GAH noo kroo-za-MAIN-too, VEE-re ah ees-KAYR-da.*

**Stay in your lane until it splits off to the right.**
Permaneça na sua faixa até que ela se divida para a direita.
*payh-ma-NAY-sa nah SOO-a FAH-ee-sha ah-TEH kee EH-la see gee-VEE-da PAH-ra ah gee-RAY-ta.*

**Don't go onto the ramp.**
Não suba a rampa.
*NANN-oo SOO-ba ah HAM-pa.*

**You are going in the wrong direction.**

Você está indo na direção errada.

*voe-SAY ees-TAH EEN-doo nah gee-ray-SAWM ay-HA-dah.*

**Can you guide me to this location?**

Você pode me explicar o caminho até esse local?

*voe-SAY POH-gee mee ays-plee-KAH oo ka-MEE-nyo ah-TEH AY-sy loe-KAW?*

**Stop at the crossroads.**

Pare no cruzamento.

*PAH-ree noo kroo-za-MAIN-too.*

**You missed our turn. Please turn around.**

Você passou direto. Faça o retorno, por favor.

*voe-SAY pah-SOE gee-REH-too. FAH-sa oo hay-TOEH-noo, poer fa-VOER.*

**It is illegal to turn here.**

Não é permitido dobrar aqui.

*NANN-oo eh payr-mee-CHEE-doo doe-BRAR ah-KEE.*

**We're lost, could you help us?**

Estamos perdidos, você pode nos ajudar?

*ees-TAM-moos payr-GEE-doos, voe-SAY POH-gee noos ah-zhoo-DAR?*

# APOLOGIES

**Dad, I'm sorry.**
Desculpa, papai.
*gees-KOO-pa, pah-PAH-ee.*

**I apologize for being late.**
Peço desculpas pelo atraso.
*PEH-soo gees-KOO-pas PAY-loo ah-TRA-zoo.*

**Excuse me for not bringing money.**
Desculpa por não ter trazido dinheiro.
*gees-KOO-pa poer NANN-oo tayh tra-ZEE-doo dee-GNAY-roo.*

**That was my fault.**
Foi culpa minha.
*foy KOO-pa MEE-nya.*

**It won't happen again, I'm sorry.**
Desculpa, não vai mais acontecer.
*gees-KOO-pa, NANN-oo VAH-ee MAH-ees ah-kon-tay-SAYH.*

**I won't break another promise.**
Não vou mais quebrar nenhuma promessa.
*NANN-oo voe MAH-ees kay-BRAH nain-GNOO-ma proe-MEH-sa.*

**You have my word that I'll be careful.**
Prometo que vou ter cuidado.
*pro-MAY-too kee voe tayh kooy-DAH-doo.*

**I'm sorry, I wasn't paying attention.**
Desculpa, eu não estava prestando atenção.
*gees-KOO-pa, AY-oo NANN-oo ees-TAH-va prays-TAN-doo ah-tayn-SAWM.*

**I regret that. I'm so sorry.**
Estou arrependido. Mil desculpas.
*ees-TOE ah-khay-pain-GEE-doo. myw gees-KOO-pas.*

**I'm sorry, but today I can't.**
Desculpa, mas hoje eu não posso.
*gees-KOO-pa, MAH-ees OE-zhee AY-oo NANN-oo POH-soo.*

**It's not your fault, I'm sorry.**
Sinto muito, não é sua culpa.
*SEEN-too MOON-ee-too, NANN-oo eh SOO-ah KOO-pa.*

**Please, give me another chance.**
Por favor, me dê outra chance.
*poer fa-VOER, mee day OE-tra SHAN-see.*

**Will you ever forgive me?**
Algum dia você vai me perdoar?
*ahw-GOOM GEE-ah voe-SAY VAH-ee mee payh-doe-AH?*

**I hope in time we can still be friends.**
Espero que possamos ser amigos de novo.
*Ays-PEH-roo kee poe-SAM-moos sayh ah-MEE-goos gee NOE-voo.*

**I screwed up, and I'm sorry.**
Eu errei, me desculpa.
*AY-oo ay-HAY, mee gees-KOO-pa.*

# SMALL TALK

**No.**
Não.
*NANN-oo.*

**Yes.**
Sim.
*seem.*

**Okay.**
Okay.
*Oh-KAY.*

**Please.**
Por favor.
*poer fa-VOER.*

**Do you fly out of the country often?**
Você sempre viaja para fora do país?
*voe-SAY SAYN-pree vee-AH-zha PAH-ra FOH-ra doo pah-EES?*

**Thank you.**
Obrigado.
*oe-bree-GAH-doo.*

**That's okay.**
Tudo bem.
*TOO-doo bayn.*

**I went shopping.**
Fui fazer compras.
*fooy fah-ZAYR KOM-pras.*

**There.**
Lá.
*lah.*

**Very well.**
Muito bem.
*MOON-ee-too bayn.*

**What?**
O quê?
*oo kay?*

**I think you'll like it.**
Acho que você vai gostar.
*AH-shoo kee voe-SAY VAH-ee goes-TAH.*

**When?**
Quando?
*KWAN-doo?*

**I didn't sleep well.**
Não dormi bem.
*NANN-oo doeh-MEE bayn.*

**Until what time?**
Até que horas?
*ah-TEH kee OH-ras?*

**We are waiting in line.**
Estamos esperando na fila.
*ees-TAM-moos ays-pay-RAN-doo nah FEE-la.*

**We're only waiting for a little bit longer.**
Vamos esperar só mais um pouco.
*VAM-moos ays-pay-RAH soh MAH-ees oom POE-koo.*

**How?**
Como?
*KOE-moo?*

**Where?**
Onde?
*OWN-gee?*

**I'm glad.**
Estou feliz.
*ees-TOE fay-LEES.*

**You are very tall.**
Você é muito alto. (masc.) | Você é muito alta. (fem.)
*voe-SAY eh MOON-ee-too AHW-too. (masc.)| voe-SAY eh MOON-ee-too AHW-ta. (fem.)*

**I like to speak your language.**
Gosto de falar o seu idioma.
*GOHS-too gee fah-LAR oo SAY-oo ee-gee-OE-ma.*

**You are very kind.**
Você é muito gentil.
*voe-SAY eh MOON-ee-too zhayn-CHEEW.*

**Happy birthday!**
Feliz Aniversário!
*fay-LEES ah-nee-vayh-SAH-ryu!*

**I would like to thank you very much.**
Quero te agradecer muito.
*KEH-roo chee ah-gra-day-SAYH MOON-ee-too.*

**Here is a gift that I bought for you.**
Esse é um presente que comprei para você.
*AY-sy eh oom pray-ZAYN-chee kee kom-PRAY PAH-ra voe-SAY.*

**Yes. Thank you for all of your help.**
Sim. Obrigado pela sua ajuda.
*seem. oe-bree-GAH-doo PAY-la SOO-a ah-ZHOO-da.*

**What did you get?**
O que você comprou?
*oo kee voe-SAY kom-PROE?*

**Have a good trip!**
Boa viagem!
*BOE-ah vy-AH-zhayn!*

**This place is very special to me.**
Esse lugar é muito especial para mim.
*AY-sy loo-GAR eh MOON-ee-too ays-pay-see-AH-oo PAH-ra meen.*

**My foot is asleep.**
Meu pé está dormente.
*MAY-oo peh ees-TAH dor-MAYN-chee.*

**May I open this now or later?**
Posso abrir agora ou depois?
*POH-soo ah-BREEH ah-GOH-ra oe day-POYS?*

**Why do you think that is?**
Por que você acha isso?
*poor-KAY voe-SAY AH-sha EE-soo?*

**Which do you like better, chocolate or caramel?**
Do que você gosta mais, chocolate ou caramelo?
*doo kee voe-SAY GOHS-ta MAH-ees, shoe-koe-LAH-chee oe kah-rah-MEH-loo?*

**Be safe on your journey.**
Tenha uma viagem segura.
*TAYN-gna OO-ma vy-AH-zhayn say-GOO-ra.*

**I want to do this for a little longer.**
Quero fazer isso um pouco mais.
*KEH-roo fah-ZAYR EE-soo oom POE-koo MAH-ees.*

**This is a picture that I took at the hotel.**
Essa é uma foto que eu tirei no hotel.
*EH-sa eh OO-ma FOH-too kee AY-oo chee-RAY noo oe-TEHW.*

**Allow me.**
Você permite?
*voe-SAY payr-MEE-chee?*

**I was surprised.**
Fiquei surpreso.
*fee-KAY soor-PRAY-zoo.*

**I like that.**
Gostei.
*goes-TAY.*

**Are you in high spirits today?**
Está de bom humor hoje?
*ees-TAH gee bown oo-MOEH OE-zhee?*

**Oh, here comes my wife.**
Ah, minha esposa está chegando.
*Ah, MEE-nya ees-POE-za ees-TAH shay-GAN-doo.*

**Can I see the photograph?**
Posso ver a foto?
*POH-soo vayh ah FOH-too?*

**Feel free to ask me anything.**
Pode me perguntar qualquer coisa.
*POH-gee mee payr-goon-TAH kwaw-KEHR KOY-za.*

**That was magnificent!**
Foi maravilhoso!
*foy mah-rah-VEE-lyoe-zoo!*

**See you some other time.**
Até mais!
*ah-TEH MAH-ees!*

**No more, please.**
Mais não, por favor.
*MAH-ees NANN-oo, poer fa-VOER.*

**Please don't use that.**
Não use isso, por favor.
*NANN-oo OO-zee EE-soo, poer fa-VOER.*

**That is very pretty.**
É muito bonito.
*eh MOON-ee-too boe-NEE-too.*

**Would you say that again?**
Você pode repetir?
*voe-SAY POH-gee hay-pay-CHEER?*

**Speak slowly.**
Fale devagar.
*FAH-ly gee-va-GAH.*

**I'm home.**
Estou em casa.
*ees-TOE ayn KA-za.*

**Is this your home?**
Essa é a sua casa?
*EH-sa eh ah SOO-a KAH-za?*

**I know a lot about the area.**
Sei bastante sobre a região.
*say bahs-TAN-chee SOE-bree ah hay-zhee-AWM.*

**Welcome back. How was your day?**
Bem-vindo de volta. Como foi o seu dia?
*bayn-VEEN-doo gee VOH-oo-ta. KOE-moo foy oo SAY-oo GEE-ahh?*

**I read every day.**
Leio todos os dias.
*LAY-oo TOE-doos oos GEE-ahhs.*

**My favorite type of book are novels by Stephen King.**
O meu tipo favorito de livro são os romances do Stephen King.
*oo MAY-oo CHEE-poo fah-voe-REE-too gee LEE-vro sawm oos hoe-MAN-sys doo Stephen King.*

**You surprised me!**
Você me surpreendeu!
*Voe-SAY mee sooh-pree-ayn-DAY-oo!*

**I am short on time, so I have to go.**
Estou com pouco tempo, preciso ir.
*ees-TOE kom POE-koo TAYM-poo, pray-SEE-zoo eer.*

**Thank you for having this conversation.**
Obrigado pela conversa.
*oe-bree-GAH-doo PAY-la kon-VEH-sa.*

**Oh, when is it?**
Ah, quando vai ser?
*Ah, KWAN-doo VAH-ee sayh?*

**This is my brother, Jeremy.**
Esse é o meu irmão, Jeremy.
*AY-sy eh oo MAY-oo eer-MAWM, JEH-re-mee.*

**That is my favorite bookstore.**
Essa é a minha livraria favorita.
*EH-sa eh ah MEE-nya lee-vra-REE-ah fah-voe-REE-ta.*

**That statue is bigger than it looks.**
Essa estátua é maior do que parece.
*EH-sa ees-TAH-too-ah eh mah-ee-OHR doo kee pah-REH-see.*

**Look at the shape of that cloud!**
Olhe para o formato dessa nuvem!
*OH-lye PAH-ra oo foer-MAH-too DEH-sa NOO-vayn!*

# BUSINESS

**I am president of the credit union.**
Sou o presidente da cooperativa de crédito.
*soe oo pray-zee-DAYN-chee dah koe-pay-rah-CHEE-va gee KREH-gee-too.*

**We are expanding in your area.**
Estamos expandindo os nossos negócios na sua região.
*ees-TAM-moos ays-pan-DEEN-doo oos nay-GOH-see-oos nah SOO-a hay-zhee-AWM.*

**I am looking for work in the agriculture field.**
Estou procurando trabalho na área da agricultura.
*ees-TOE pro-koo-RAN-doo trah-BAH-lyo nah AH-rya dah ah-gree-koo-TOO-ra.*

**Sign here, please.**
Assine aqui, por favor.
*ah-SEEN-nee ah-KEE, poer fa-VOER.*

**I am looking for temporary work.**
Estou procurando um trabalho temporário.
*ees-TOE pro-koo-RAN-doo oom trah-BAH-lyo teim-poe-RAH-ryo.*

**I need to call and set up that meeting.**
Preciso ligar e agendar essa reunião.
*pray-SEE-zoo lee-GAR y ah-zhayn-DAH EH-sa hay-oo-nee-AWM.*

**Is the line open?**
A linha é aberta?
*eh LEE-gna eh ah-BEHR-ta?*

**I need you to hang up the phone.**
Preciso que você fique no telefone.
*pray-SEE-zoo kee voe-SAY FEE-ky noo tay-lay-FOE-nee.*

**Who should I ask for more information about your business?**
A quem devo pedir mais informações sobre a sua empresa?

ah kayn DAY-voo pay-GEEH MAH-ees een-foeh-mah-SONN-ees SOE-bree ah SOO-a aim-PRAY-za?

**There was no answer when you handed me the phone.**
Quando você me deu o telefone, ninguém falou nada.
KWAN-doo voe-SAY mee DAY-oo oo tay-lay-FOE-nee, neen-GAYN fah-LOE NAH-da.

**Robert is not here at the moment.**
O Robert não está aqui no momento.
oo HOH-beht NANN-oo ees-TAH ah-KEE noo moe-MAIN-too.

**Call me after work, thanks.**
Me liga depois do trabalho, obrigado.
mee LEE-ga day-POYS doo trah-BAH-lyo, oe-bree-GAH-doo.

**We're strongly considering your contract offer.**
Estamos considerando a sua proposta.
ees-TAM-moos kon-see-day-RAN-doo ah SOO-a proe-POHS-ta.

**Have the necessary forms been signed yet?**
Os formulários necessários já foram preenchidos?
oos foeh-moo-LAH-ryos nay-say-SAH-ryos zha foh-RAM pray-ayn-SHEE-doos?

**I have a few hours available after work.**
Tenho algumas horas disponíveis depois do trabalho.
TAYN-gnoo ahw-GOOM-as OH-ras gees-poe-NEE-vays day-POYS doo trah-BAH-lyo.

**What do they make there?**
O que fazem lá?
oo kee FAH-zain lah?

**I have no tasks assigned to me.**
Não tenho nenhuma tarefa atribuída a mim.
NANN-oo TAYN-gnoo nain-GNOO-ma tah-REH-fa ah-tree-boo-EE-dah ah meen.

**How many workers are they hiring?**
Quantas pessoas eles estão contratando?
KWAN-tas pay-SOE-ahs AY-lys ees-TAWM kon-tra-TAN-doo?

**It should take me three hours to complete this task.**
Devo levar três horas pra terminar esta tarefa.
*DAY-voo lay-VAH trays OH-ras prah tayh-mee-NAH EHS-ta tah-REH-fa.*

**Don't use that computer, it is only for financial work.**
Não use esse computador, ele é só para as questões financeiras.
*NANN-oo OO-zy AY-sy kom-poo-ta-DOEH, AY-ly eh soh PAH-ra ahs kays-TOYNS fee-nan-SAY-ras.*

**I only employ people that I can rely on.**
Só contrato pessoas em quem eu posso confiar.
*soh kon-TRAH-too pay-SOE-ahs ayn kayn AY-oo POH-soo kon-fee-AH.*

**After I talk to my lawyers, we can discuss this further.**
Depois de conversar com os meus advogados, podemos discutir isso um pouco mais.
*day-POYS gee kon-vayh-SAH kom oos MAY-oos ah-gee-voe-GAH-doos, po-DAY-moos gees-koo-CHEEH EE-soo oom POE-koo MAH-ees.*

**Are there any open positions in my field?**
Tem alguma vaga aberta na minha área?
*tayn ahw-GOOM-ah VAH-ga ah-BEHR-ta nah MEE-nya AH-rya?*

**I'll meet you in the conference room.**
Te vejo na sala de conferência.
*chee VAY-zhoo nah SAH-la gee kon-fay-RAIN-sya.*

**Call and leave a message on my office phone.**
Ligue e deixe uma mensagem no meu telefone comercial.
*LEE-ghee y DAY-shee OO-ma main-SAH-zhain noo MAY-oo tay-lay-FOE-nee koe-may-see-AHW.*

**Send me a fax with that information.**
Me envie um fax com essa informação.
*mee ayn-VEE oom fax kom EH-sa een-foeh-mah-SAWM.*

**Hi, I would like to leave a message for Sheila.**
Oi, eu gostaria de deixar uma mensagem para a Sheila.
*OE-y, AY-oo goes-ta-REE-a gee day-SHAR OO-ma main-SAH-zhain PAH-ra ah SHAY-la.*

**Please repeat your last name.**
Você pode repetir o seu último nome?
*voe-SAY POH-gee hay-pay-CHEER oo SAY-oo OO-chee-moo NOE-me?*

**I would like to buy wholesale.**
Eu gostaria de fazer uma compra por atacado.
*AY-oo goes-ta-REE-a gee fah-ZAYR OO-ma KOM-prah poeh ah-ta-KA-doo.*

**How do you spell your last name?**
Como se pronuncia o seu sobrenome?
*KOE-moo see proe-noon-SEE-ah oo SAY-oo soe-bray-NOE-me?*

**I called your boss yesterday and left a message.**
Liguei para o seu chefe ontem e deixei uma mensagem.
*LEE-gay PAH-ra oo SAY-oo SHEH-fee OWN-tayn y day-SHAY OO-ma main-SAH-zhain.*

**That customer hung up on me.**
Esse cliente acabou de desligar.
*AY-sy klee-AYN-chee ah-ka-BOE gee days-lee-GAR.*

**She called but didn't leave a callback number.**
Ela ligou, mas não deixou o número para retornarmos.
*EH-la lee-GOE, MAH-ees NANN-oo day-SHOW oo NOO-may-roo PAH-ra hay-toeh-NAH-moos.*

**Hello! Am I speaking to Bob?**
Alô! É o Bob que tá falando?
*ah-LOE! eh oo Bob kee tah fah-LAN-doo?*

**Excuse me, but could you speak up? I can't hear you.**
Desculpa, mas você pode falar um pouco mais alto? Não consigo te ouvir.
*gees-KOO-pa, MAH-ees voe-SAY POH-gee fah-LAR oom POE-koo MAH-ees AHW-too? NANN-oo kon-SEE-goo chee OE-veeh.*

**The line is very bad, could you move to a different area so I can hear you better?**
A ligação está muito ruim, você poderia ir para um lugar diferente, para que eu possa te ouvir melhor?
*ah lee-gah-SAWM ees-TAH MOON-ee-too hoo-EEN, voe-SAY poe-DAY-ree-a eer PAH-ra oom loo-GAR gee-fay-RENN-chee, PAH-ra kee AY-oo POH-sa chee oe-VEEH may-LYOR?*

**I would like to apply for a work visa.**
Eu gostaria de me candidatar a um visto de trabalho.
*AY-oo goes-ta-REE-a gee mee kan-gee-dah-TAH ah oom VEES-too gee trah-BAH-lyo.*

**It is my dream to work here teaching the language.**
É o meu sonho trabalhar aqui ensinando o idioma.
*eh oo MAY-oo SOE-gnoo tra-ba-LYAR ah-KEE ayn-see-NAN-doo oo ee-gee-OE-ma.*

**I have always wanted to work here.**
Eu sempre quis trabalhar aqui.
*EH-oo SAYN-pree kees tra-ba-LYAR ah-KEE.*

**Where do you work?**
Onde você trabalha?
*OWN-gee voe-SAY tra-BAH-lya?*

**Are we in the same field of work?**
Somos da mesma área de trabalho?
*SOE-moos dah MAYZ-ma AH-rya gee trah-BAH-lyo?*

**Do we share an office?**
Estamos no mesmo escritório?
*ees-TAM-moos noo MAYS-moo ays-kree-TOH-ree-oo?*

**What do you do for a living?**
O que você faz da vida?
*oo kee voe-SAY FAH-ees dah VEE-da?*

**I work in the city as an engineer for Cosco.**
Trabalho na cidade como engenheiro para a Cosco.
*trah-BAH-lyo nah see-DAH-gee KOE-moo ayn-zhayn-GNAY-roo PAH-ra ah KOES-koo.*

**I am an elementary teacher.**
Sou professor infantil.
*soe proe-fay-SOER een-fan-CHEE-oo.*

**What time should I be at the meeting?**
Que horas eu devo ir para a reunião?
*kee OH-ras AY-oo DAY-voo eer PAH-ra ah hay-oo-nee-AWM?*

**Would you like me to catch you up on what the meeting was about?**
Quer que eu te atualize sobre o assunto da reunião?
*kehr kee AY-oo chee ah-too-ah-LEE-zee SOE-bree oo ah-SOON-too dah hay-oo-nee-AWM?*

**I would like to set up a meeting with your company.**
Eu gostaria de marcar uma reunião com a empresa de vocês.
*AY-oo goes-ta-REE-a gee mar-KAR OO-ma hay-oo-nee-AWM kom ah aim-PRAY-za gee voe-SAYS.*

**Please, call my secretary for that information.**
Por favor, ligue para a minha secretária para pedir essa informação.
*poer fa-VOER, LEE-ghee PAH-ra ah MEE-nya say-kray-TAH-ree-ah PAH-ra pay-GEEH EH-sa een-foeh-mah-SAWM.*

**I will have to ask my lawyer.**
Vou ter que perguntar ao meu advogado.
*voe tayh kee payr-goon-TAH AH-oo MAY-oo ah-gee-voe-GAH-doo.*

**Fax it over to my office number.**
Envie um fax para o número do meu escritório.
*ayn-VEE-ee oom fax PAH-ra oo NOO-may-roo doo MAY-oo ays-kree-TOH-ree-oo.*

**Will I have any trouble calling into the office?**
Vou ter algum problema para ligar para o escritório?
*voe tayh ahw-GOOM proe-BLAY-mah PAH-ra lee-GAR PAH-ra oo ays-kree-TOH-ree-oo?*

**Do you have a business card I can have?**
Você tem algum cartão de visitas para me dar?
*voe-SAY tayn ahw-GOOM kah-TAWM gee vee-ZEE-tas PAH-ra mee dah?*

**Here is my business card. Please, take it.**
Aqui está o meu cartão de visitas. Fique com ele, por favor.
*ah-KEE ees-TAH oo MAY-oo kah-TAWM gee vee-ZEE-tas. FEE-ky kom AY-ly, poer fa-VOER.*

**My colleague and I are going to lunch.**
Eu e meu colega vamos almoçar.
*AY-oo y MAY-oo koe-LEH-ga VAM-moos ah-oo-moe-SAH.*

**I am the director of finance for my company.**
Sou o Diretor Financeiro da minha empresa.
*soe oo gee-ray-TOEH fee-nan-SAY-roo dah MEE-nya aim-PRAY-za.*

**I manage the import goods of my company.**
Sou responsável pelas importações da minha empresa.

*soe hays-pon-SAH-vew PAY-las eem-poeh-tah-SOWN-ees dah MEE-nya aim-PRAY-za.*

**My colleagues' boss is Steven.**
O chefe dos meus colegas é o Steven.
*oo SHEH-fee MAY-oos koe-LEH-gas eh oo Steven.*

**I work for the gas station company.**
Trabalho para a empresa do posto de combustível.
*trah-BAH-lyo PAH-ra ah aim-PRAY-za doo POES-too gee kom-boos-CHEE-vew.*

**What company do you work for?**
Você trabalha para qual empresa?
*voe-SAY trah-BAH-lya PAH-ra kwaw aim-PRAY-za?*

**I'm an independent contractor.**
Sou terceirizado.
*soe tayh-say-ree-ZAH-doo.*

**How many employees do you have at your company?**
Quantos funcionários tem na sua empresa?
*KWAN-toos foon-sy-oe-NAH-ryos tayn nah SOO-a aim-PRAY-za?*

**I know a lot about engineering.**
Sei bastante sobre engenharia.
*say bahs-TAN-chee SOE-bree ain-zhein-ah-REE-ah.*

**I can definitely resolve that dispute for you.**
Com certeza posso ajudar a resolver esse conflito.
*kom sayr-TAY-za POH-soo ah-zhoo-DAR ah hay-zoe-VAYH AY-sy kon-FLEE-too.*

**You should hire an interpreter.**
Vocês deveriam contratar um intérprete.
*voe-SAYS day-vay-RI-am kon-tra-TAH oom een-TEH-pray-chee.*

**Are you hiring any additional workers?**
Vocês estão contratando mais funcionários?
*voe-SAYS ees-TAWM kon-tra-TAN-doo MAH-ees foon-sy-oe-NAH-ryos?*

**How much experience do I need to work here?**
Quanto tempo de experiência eu preciso para trabalhar aqui?

*KWAN-too TAYM-poo gee ays-pay-ree-AYN-sya AY-oo pray-SEE-zoo PAH-ra tra-ba-LYAR ah-KEE?*

**Our marketing manager handles that.**
O nosso gerente de marketing cuida disso.
*oo NOH-soo zhay-RAYN-chee gee MAHH-kay-cheen KOOY-da DEE-soo.*

**I would like to poach one of your workers.**
Eu gostaria de roubar um dos seus funcionários.
*AY-oo goes-ta-REE-a gee hoe-BAH oo doos SAY-oos foon-sy-oe-NAH-ryos.*

**Can we work out a deal that is beneficial for the both of us?**
Podemos fechar um negócio que seja benéfico para os dois lados?
*po-DAY-moos fay-SHAH oom nay-GOH-syo kee SAY-zha bay-NEH-fee-koo PAH-ra oos doys LAH-doos?*

**My resources are at your disposal.**
Os meus recursos estão à sua disposição.
*oos MAY-oos hay-KOOH-soos ays-TAWM ah SOO-ah gees-poe-zee-SAWM.*

**I am afraid that we have to let you go.**
Talvez tenhamos que te desligar.
*tahw-VAYS tain-AH-moose kee chee days-lee-GAR.*

**This is your first warning. Please don't do that again.**
Essa é a sua primeira advertência. Por favor, não faça isso de novo.
*EH-sa eh ah SOO-a pree-MAY-ra ah-gee-vayh-TAYN-sya. poer fa-VOER, NANN-oo FAH-sa EE-soo gee NOE-voo.*

**File a complaint with HR about the incident.**
Relate o incidente ao RH.
*hay-LAH-chee oo een-sy-DAYN-chee AH-oo EH-hee ah-GAH.*

**Who is showing up for our lunch meeting?**
Quem vai aparecer para a nossa reunião de almoço?
*kayn VAH-ee ah-pah-ray-SAYH PAH-ra ah NOH-sa hay-oo-nee-AWM gee ahw-MOE-soo?*

**Clear out the rest of my day.**
Libera o resto do meu dia.
*lee-BEH-ra oo HES-too doo MAY-oo GEE-ah.*

**We need to deposit this into the bank.**
Precisamos depositar isso no banco.
*pray-see-ZAM-moos day-poe-zee-TAH EE-soo noo BAN-koo.*

**Can you cover the next hour for me?**
Você pode me cobrir durante a próxima hora?
*voe-SAY POH-gee mee koe-BREEH doo-RANN-chee ah PROH-see-ma OH-ra?*

**If Shania calls, please push her directly through.**
Se a Shania ligar, pode me encaminhar a ligação.
*see ah Shania lee-GAR, POH-gee mee ayn-ka-meen-NYAR ah lee-gah-SAWM.*

**I'm leaving early today.**
Vou sair mais cedo hoje.
*voe sah-EEH MAH-ees SAY-doo OE-zhee.*

**I'll be working late tonight.**
Vou trabalhar até mais tarde hoje.
*voe tra-ba-LYAR ah-TEH MAH-ees TAR-gee OE-zhee.*

**You can use the bathroom in my office.**
Pode usar o banheiro do meu escritório.
*POH-gee oo-ZAR oo bahn-GNAY-roo doo MAY-oo ays-kree-TOH-ree-oo.*

**You can use my office phone to call out.**
Pode usar o telefone do meu escritório.
*POH-gee oo-ZAR oo tay-lay-FOE-nee doo MAY-oo ays-kree-TOH-ree-oo.*

**Please, close the door behind you.**
Por favor, feche a porta atrás de você.
*poer fa-VOER, FAY-shy ah POH-ta ah-TRAH-ys gee voe-SAY.*

**I need to talk to you privately.**
Preciso falar com você em particular.
*pray-SEE-zoo fah-LAR kom voe-SAY ayn pah-chee-koo-LAH.*

**Your team is doing good work on this project.**
A sua equipe está fazendo um bom trabalho nesse projeto.
*ah SOO-a ay-KEE-pee ees-TAH fah-ZAIN-doo oom bown trah-BAH-lyo NAY-sy proe-ZHEH-too.*

**Our numbers are down this quarter.**
Os nossos números estão ruins nesse trimestre.
*oos NOH-soos NOO-may-roos ees-TAWM hoo-EENS NAY-sy tree-MEHS-tree.*

**I need you to work harder than usual.**
Preciso que você trabalhe mais do que o normal.
*pray-SEE-zoo kee voe-SAY trah-BAH-lye MAH-ees doo kee oo nor-MAHW.*

**I'm calling in sick today. Can anyone cover my shift?**
Estou doente hoje. Alguém pode me substituir?
*ees-TOE doe-AIN-chee OE-zhee. AHW-gain POH-gee mee soobs-chee-too-EEH?*

**Tom, we are thinking of promoting you.**
Tom, estamos pensando em te promover.
*Tom, ees-TAM-moos pain-SAN-doo ayn chee proe-moe-VAYH.*

**I would like a raise.**
Eu gostaria de ganhar um aumento.
*AY-oo goes-ta-REE-a gee gann-GNAR oom ah-oo-MAIN-too.*

# THE WEATHER

**I think the weather is changing.**
Acho que o tempo está mudando.
*AH-shoo kee oo TAYM-poo ees-TAH moo-DAN-doo.*

**Be careful, it is raining outside.**
Cuidado, está chovendo lá fora.
*kooy-DAH-doo, ees-TAH shoo-VAIN-doo lah FOH-ra.*

**Make sure to bring your umbrella**
Traga o seu guarda-chuva.
*TRA-ga oo SAY-oo GWAH-da SHOO-va.*

**Get out of the rain or you will catch a cold.**
Saia da chuva para não pegar um resfriado.
*SAH-ya dah SHOO-va PAH-ra NANN-oo pay-GAH oom hays-free-AH-doo.*

**Is it snowing?**
Está nevando?
*ees-TAH nay-VAN-doo?*

**The snow is very thick right now.**
A neve está muito grossa agora.
*ah NEH-vee ees-TAH MOON-ee-too GROH-sa ah-GOH-ra.*

**Be careful, the road is full of ice.**
Cuidado, a estrada está cheia de gelo.
*kooy-DAH-doo, ah ees-TRA-da ees-TAH SHAY-ah gee ZHAY-loo.*

**What is the climate like here? Is it warm or cold?**
Como é o clima aqui? É quente ou frio?
*KOE-moo eh oo KLEE-ma ah-KEE? Eh KAYN-chee oe FREE-oo?*

**It has been a very nice temperature here.**
A temperatura está muito boa aqui.
*ah tayn-pay-ra-TOO-ra ees-TAH MOON-ee-too BOE-a ah-KEE.*

**Does it rain a lot here?**
Chove muito aqui?
*SHOH-vee MOON-ee-too ah-KEE?*

**The temperature is going to break records this week.**
A temperatura vai bater recorde essa semana.
*ah tayn-peh-rah-TOO-ra VAH-ee bah-TAYH heh-KOH-gee EH-sa say-MANN-na.*

**Does it ever snow here?**
Aqui tem neve?
*ah-KEE tayn NEH-vee?*

**When does it get sunny?**
Quando fica mais ensolarado?
*KWAN-doo FEE-ka MAH-ees ayn-soe-la-RAH-doo?*

**What's the forecast look like for tomorrow?**
Qual é a previsão do tempo para amanhã?
*kwaw eh ah pray-vee-ZAWM doo TAYM-poo PAH-ra ah-man-GNAN?*

**This is a heatwave.**
Essa é uma onda de calor.
*EH-sa eh OO-ma OWN-da gee kah-LOEH.*

**Right now, it is overcast, but it should clear up by this evening.**
Agora está nublado, mas o tempo vai abrir mais à noite.
*ah-GOH-ra ees-TAH MAH-ees noo-BLAH-doo, MAH-ees oo TAYM-poo VAH-ee ah-BREEH MAH-ees ah NOY-chee.*

**It is going to heat up in the afternoon.**
Vai esquentar à tarde.
*VAH-ee ees-kayn-TAH ah TAR-gee.*

**What channel is the weather channel?**
Em qual canal eu posso ver a previsão do tempo?
*ayn kwaw kan-NAW AY-oo POH-soo vayh ah pray-vee-ZAWM doo TAYM-poo?*

**Tonight it will be below freezing.**
Vai ter geada hoje à noite.
*VAH-ee tayh zhay-AH-da OE-zhee ah NOY-chee.*

**It's very windy outside.**

Está ventando lá fora.

*ees-TAH vain-TAN-doo lah FOH-ra.*

**It's going to be cold in the morning.**

Vai esfriar de manhã.

*VAH-ee ees-free-AH gee man-GNAN.*

**It's not raining, only drizzling.**

Não está chovendo, só chuviscando.

*NANN-oo ees-TAH shoo-VAIN-doo, soh shoo-vees-KAN-doo.*

# HOTEL

**I would like to book a room.**
Gostaria de reservar um quarto.
*goes-ta-REE-a gee hay-zayh-VAH oom KWAR-too.*

**I'd like a single room.**
Gostaria de um quarto individual.
*goes-ta-REE-a gee oom KWAR-too een-gee-vee-doo-AH-oo.*

**I'd like a suite.**
Gostaria de uma suíte.
*goes-ta-REE-a gee OO-ma soo-EE-chee.*

**How much is the room per night?**
Qual é o preço do quarto, por noite?
*kwaw eh oo PRAY-soo doo KWAR-too, poeh NOY-chee?*

**How much is the room with tax?**
Qual é o preço do quarto, incluindo as taxas?
*kwaw eh oo PRAY-soo doo KWAR-too een-kloo-EEN-doo ahs TAH-shas?*

**When is the checkout time?**
Qual é a hora do checkout?
*kwaw eh ah OH-ra doo checkout?*

**I'd like a room with a nice view.**
Gostaria de um quarto que tenha uma vista bonita.
*goes-ta-REE-a gee oom KWAR-too kee TAYN-gna OO-ma VEES-ta boe-NEE-ta.*

**I'd like to order room service.**
Gostaria de pedir serviço de quarto.
*goes-ta-REE-a gee pay-GEEH sayr-VEE-soo gee KWAR-too.*

**Let's go swim in the outdoor pool.**
Vamos nadar na piscina do lado de fora.
*VAM-moos na-DAH nah pee-SEE-na doo LAH-doo gee FOH-ra.*

**Are pets allowed at the hotel?**
É permitido animal de estimação no hotel?
*eh payr-mee-CHEE-doo ah-nee-MAHW gee ays-chee-mah-SAWM noo oe-TEHW?*

**I would like a room on the first floor.**
Gostaria de um quarto no primeiro andar.
*goes-ta-REE-a gee oom KWAR-too noo pree-MAY-roo an-DAH.*

**Can you send maintenance up to our room for a repair?**
Você pode mandar a manutenção subir para fazer um reparo?
*voe-SAY POH-gee man-DAH ah man-noo-tayn-SAWM soo-BEEH PAH-ra fah-ZAYR oom hay-PAH-roo?*

**I'm locked out of my room, could you unlock it?**
Estou preso fora do quarto, você pode abrir a porta?
*ees-TOE PRAY-zoo FOH-ra doo KWAR-too, voe-SAY POH-gee ah-BREEH ah POHR-ta?*

**Our door is jammed and won't open.**
A nossa porta está emperrada e não quer abrir.
*ah NOH-sa POHR-ta ees-TAH ain-pay-HA-dah y NANN-oo kehr ah-BREEH.*

**How do you work the shower?**
Como funciona o chuveiro?
*KOE-moo foon-see-OE-na oo shoo-VAY-roo?*

**Are the consumables in the room free?**
Os produtos disponíveis no quarto são gratuitos?
*oos proe-DOO-toos gees-poe-NEE-vays noo KWAR-too sawm gra-TOOY-toos?*

**What is my final bill for the stay, including incidentals?**
Quanto é a minha conta geral da estadia, incluindo os extras?
*KWAN-too eh ah MEE-nya KON-ta gay-rau dah ays-tah-DEE-ah een-kloo-EEN-doo oos AYS-tras?*

**Can you show me to my room?**
Você pode me mostrar o quarto?
*voe-SAY POH-gee mee moes-TRAH oo KWAR-too?*

**Where can I get ice for my room?**
Onde posso pegar gelo para o meu quarto?
*OWN-gee POH-soo pay-GAH ZHAY-loo PAH-ra oo MAY-oo KWAR-too?*

**Do you have any rooms available?**
Vocês têm quartos disponíveis?
*voe-SAYS tayn KWAR-toos gees-poe-NEE-vays?*

**Do you sell bottled water?**
Vocês vendem água em garrafa?
*voe-SAYS vayn-DAYN AH-gwa ayn gah-HA-fa?*

**Our towels are dirty.**
As nossas toalhas estão sujas.
*ahs NOH-sas toe-AH-lyas ees-TAWM SOO-zhas.*

**Have you stayed at this hotel before?**
Você já se hospedou nesse hotel antes?
*voe-SAY zha see oes-pay-DOE NAY-sy oe-TEHW AHN-chees?*

**How much is a room for two adults?**
Quanto é o quarto para dois adultos?
*KWAN-too eh oo KWAR-too PAH-ra doys ah-DOO-toos?*

**Does the room come with a microwave?**
Tem microondas no quarto?
*tayn mee-kroe-ON-das noo KWAR-too?*

**May I see the room first? That way I will know if I like it.**
Posso ver o quarto primeiro? Para ver se eu gosto.
*POH-soo vayh oo KWAR-too pree-MAY-roo? PAH-ra vayh see AY-oo GOHS-too.*

**Do you have a room that is quieter?**
Vocês têm algum quarto mais silencioso?
*voe-SAYS tayn ahw-GOOM KWAR-too MAH-ees see-layn-see-OE-zoo?*

**How much is the deposit for my stay?**
Quanto custa a reserva da minha estadia?
*KWAN-too KOOS-ta ah hay-ZEH-va dah MEE-nya ays-tah-GEE-ah?*

**Is the tap water drinkable at the hotel?**
A água da torneira do hotel é potável?
*ah AH-gwa da toer-NAY-ra doo oe-TEHW eh poe-TAH-vew?*

**Will there be any holds on my credit card?**
Vai precisar deixar algum valor reservado no meu cartão de crédito?

*VAH-ee pray-see-ZAR day-SHAR ahw-GOOM vah-LOEH hay-zayh-VAH-doo noo MAY-oo kah-TAWM gee KREH-gee-too?*

**Can I get a replacement room key?**
Posso ficar com uma chave reserva?
*POH-soo fee-KAR kom OO-ma SHA-vee hay-ZEH-va?*

**How much is a replacement room key?**
Quanto custa a chave reserva para o quarto?
*KWAN-too KOOS-ta ah SHA-vee hay-ZEH-va PAH-ra oo KWAR-too?*

**Does the bathroom have a shower or a bathtub?**
O banheiro tem chuveiro ou banheira?
*oo bahn-GNAY-roo tayn shoo-VAY-roo oe bahn-GNAY-ra?*

**Are any of the channels on the TV available in English?**
Tem algum canal na TV disponível em inglês?
*tayn ahw-GOOM ka-NAW gees-poe-NEE-vew ayn een-GLAYS?*

**I want a bigger room.**
Quero um quarto maior.
*KEH-roo oom KWAR-too mah-ee-OHR.*

**Do you serve breakfast in the morning?**
Vocês servem café-da-manhã?
*voe-SAYS SEH-vayn ka-FEH dah man-GNAN?*

**Oh, it's spacious.**
Ah, é grande.
*Ah, eh GRAN-gee.*

**My room is this way.**
O meu quarto é por aqui.
*oo MAY-oo KWAR-too eh poer ah-KEE.*

**Straight down the hall.**
No final do corredor.
*noo fy-NAW doo koe-hay-DOER.*

**Can you suggest a different hotel?**
Você pode sugerir outro hotel?
*voe-SAY POH-gee soo-zhay-REEH OE-troo oe-TEHW?*

**Does the room have a safe for my valuables?**
O quarto tem um cofre para as coisas de valor?
*oo KWAR-too tayn oom KOH-free PAH-ra as KOY-zas gee vah-LOEH?*

**Please clean my room.**
Limpe o meu quarto, por favor.
*LEEM-pee oo MAY-oo KWAR-too, poer fa-VOER.*

**Don't disturb me, please.**
Por favor não me incomode.
*poer fa-VOER NANN-oo mee een-koe-MOH-gee.*

**Can you wake me up at noon?**
Você pode me acordar ao meio-dia?
*voe-SAY POH-gee mee ah-koeh-DAH AH-oo MAY-oo GEE-ahh?*

**I would like to check out of my hotel room.**
Gostaria de fazer o checkout.
*goes-ta-REE-a gee fah-ZAYR oo checkout.*

**Please increase the cleanup duty of my hotel room.**
Por favor, peça mais limpeza para o meu quarto.
*poer fa-VOER, PEH-sa MAH-ees leem-PAY-za PAH-ra oo MAY-oo KWAR-too.*

**Is the Marriott any good?**
O Marriott é bom?
*oo Marriott eh bown?*

**Is it expensive to stay at the Marriott?**
A hospedagem no Marriott é cara?
*ah oes-pay-DAH-zhayn noo Marriott eh KAH-ra?*

**I think our room has bedbugs.**
Acho que tem ácaro no nosso quarto.
*AH-shoo kee tayn AH-ka-roo noo NOH-soo KWAR-too.*

**Can you send an exterminator to our room?**
Você pode mandar um inseticida para o nosso quarto?
*voe-SAY POH-gee man-DAH oom een-seh-chee-SEE-da PAH-ra oo NOH-soo KWAR-too?*

**I need to speak to your manager.**
Preciso falar com o gerente.
*pray-SEE-zoo fah-LAR kom oo zhay-RAYN-chee.*

**Do you have the number to corporate?**
Você tem o número da gerência?
*voe-SAY tayn oo NOO-may-roo da zhay-RAYN-sya?*

**Does the hotel shuttle go to the casino?**
O hotel tem transporte para o cassino?
*oo oe-TEHW tayn trans-POH-chee PAH-ra oo kah-SEE-noo?*

**Can you call me when the hotel shuttle is on its way?**
Você pode ligar para mim quando o transporte do hotel estiver a caminho?
*voe-SAY POH-gee lee-GAR PAH-ra meen KWAN-doo oo trans-POH-chee doo oe-TEHW ays-chee-VEH ah ka-MEEN-gnyo?*

**Can we reserve this space for a party?**
Podemos reservar esse espaço para uma festa?
*po-DAY-moos hay-zayh-VAH AY-sy ees-PAH-soo PAH-ra OO-ma FEHS-tah?*

**What is the guest limit for reserving an area?**
Qual é o limite de convidados para a reserva de um espaço?
*kwaw eh oo lee-MEE-chee gee kon-vee-DAH-doos PAH-ra ah hay-ZEH-va gee oom ees-PAH-soo?*

**What are the rules for reserving an area?**
Quais são as regras para reservar um espaço?
*KWA-ees sawm ahs HEH-gras PAH-ra hay-zayh-VAH oom ees-PAH-soo?*

**Can we serve or drink alcohol during our get together?**
Podemos servir e consumir álcool durante a nossa festa?
*po-DAY-moos sayr-VEER y kon-soo-MEER AHW-koe doo-RANN-chee ah NOH-sa FEHS-tah?*

**I would like to complain about a noisy room next to us.**
Gostaria de reclamar sobre um quarto barulhento perto de nós.
*goes-ta-REE-a gee hay-kla-MAR SOE-bree oom KWAR-too bah-roo-LYEN-too PEHR-too gee NOH-ys.*

**We have some personal items missing from our room.**
Estamos sentindo falta de alguns itens pessoais no nosso quarto.
*ees-TAM-moos sain-TEEN-doo FAHW-ta gee ahw-GOON-s EE-tayns pay-soe-AHYS noo NOH-soo KWAR-too.*

# SPORTS AND EXERCISE

**Can we walk faster?**
Vamos caminhar mais rápido?
*VAM-moos ka-mee-NYAR MAH-ees HAH-pee-doo?*

**Do you want to go to a drag race track?**
Quer ir assistir a uma corrida de carros?
*kehr eer ah-sees-CHEEH ah OO-ma koe-HEE-da gee KAH-hoos?*

**Are you taking a walk?**
Está dando um passeio?
*ees-TAH DAN-doo oom pah-SAY-oo?*

**Do you want to jog for a kilometer or two?**
Quer correr por um ou dois quilômetros?
*kehr koe-HAYH poer oom oe doys kee-LOE-meh-troos?*

**How about fast walking?**
O que acha de andarmos rápido?
oo kee *AH-sha gee an-DAH-moos HAH-pee-doo?*

**Would you like to walk with me?**
Quer caminhar comigo?
*kehr ka-mee-NYAR ko-MEE-goo?*

**He is a really good player.**
Ele é um ótimo jogador.
*AY-ly eh oom OH-chee-moo zhoe-gah-DOEH.*

**I feel bad that they traded him to the other team.**
Que pena que venderam ele para o outro time.
*kee PAY-na kee vayn-DAY-ram AY-lee PAH-ra oo OE-troo CHEE-me.*

**Did you see that home run?**
Você viu aquela jogada?
*voe-SAY veew ah-KEH-la zhoe-GAH-da?*

**I have been a fan of that team for many years.**
Sou fã desse time há muitos anos.
*soe fann DAY-sy CHEE-me ah MOON-ee-toos ANN-noos.*

**Who is your favorite team?**
Qual é o seu time favorito?
*kwaw eh oo SAY-oo CHEE-me fah-voe-REE-too?*

**Pelé is my favorite player.**
O meu jogador preferido é o Pelé.
*oo MAY-oo zhoe-gah-DOEH pray-fay-REE-doo eh oo pay-LEH.*

**Do you like soccer?**
Você gosta de futebol?
*voe-SAY GOHS-ta gee foo-chee-BALL?*

**Do you watch American football?**
Você assiste futebol americano?
*Voe-SAY ah-SEES-chee foo-chee-BALL ah-may-ree-KAN-noo?*

**Are there any games on right now?**
Tem algum jogo passando agora?
*tayn ahw-GOOM ZHOE-goo pah-SAN-doo ah-GOH-ra?*

**That was a bad call by the ref.**
O juiz errou.
*oo zhoo-EES ay-HOE.*

**I put a lot of money on this game.**
Coloquei muita grana nesse jogo.
*koe-loe-KAY MOON-ee-ta GRAN-na NAY-sy ZHOE-goo.*

**His stats have been incredible this season.**
O desempenho dele foi incrível nesse campeonato.
*oo day-zaym-PAYN-gnoo DAY-ly foy een-KREE-vew NAY-sy kam-pay-oe-NAH-too.*

**Do you want to play baseball today?**
Quer jogar baseball hoje?
*kehr zhoe-GAR baseball OE-zhee?*

**Let's go to the soccer field and practice.**
Vamos para o campo de futebol e praticar.
*VAM-moos PAH-ra oo KAM-poo gee foo-chee-BALL y prah-chee-KAH.*

**I am barely working up a sweat.**
Quase não estou suando.
*KWAH-zee NANN-oo ees-TOE soo-AN-doo.*

**Let's go to the gym and lift weights.**
Vamos para a academia pegar uns pesos.
*VAM-moos PAH-ra ah ah-ka-day-MEE-ah pay-GAH oons PAY-zoos.*

**Give me more weights.**
Me dá mais pesos.
*mee dah MAH-ees PAY-zoos.*

**Take some weights off.**
Tira um pouco de peso.
*CHEE-ra oom POE-koo gee PAY-zoo.*

**Will you spot me?**
Pode me ajudar?
*POH-gee mee ah-zhoo-DAR?*

**How long do you want me to run on the treadmill?**
Devo correr na esteira por quanto tempo?
*DAY-voo koe-HAYH nah ees-TAY-ra pooh KWAN-too TAYM-poo?*

**Is this the best gym in the area?**
Essa é a melhor academia na região?
*EH-sa eh ah may-LYOR ah-ka-day-MEE-ah nah hay-zhee-AWM?*

**Do I need a membership to enter this gym?**
Preciso fazer matrícula para entrar nessa academia?
*pray-SEE-zoo fah-ZAYR mah-TREE-koo-la PAH-ra ayn-TRAH NEH-sa ah-ka-day-MEE-a?*

**Do you have trial memberships for tourists?**
Vocês têm planos diários para turistas?
*voe-SAYS tayn PLANN-noos dee-AH-ree-ous PAH-ra too-REES-tas?*

**My muscles are still sore from the last workout.**
Os meus músculos ainda estão doendo por causa do último treino.
*oos MAY-oos MOOS-koo-loos ah-EEN-da ees-TAWM doe-AIN-doo poeh KAW-za doo TRAY-noo.*

**Give me a second while I adjust this.**
Me dá um segundo, enquanto eu conserto isso.
*mee dah oom say-GOON-doo, ain-KWAN-too AY-oo kon-SEH-too EE-soo.*

**Time to hit the steam room!**
Hora de dar uma passada na sauna!
*OH-ra gee dah OO-ma pah-SAH-da nah SAH-oo-na!*

**You can put that in my locker.**
Pode deixar isso no meu armário.
*POH-gee day-SHAR EE-soo noo MAY-oo ar-MAH-ryo.*

**I think we have to take turns on this machine.**
Acho que precisamos revezar nessa máquina.
*AH-shoo kee pray-see-ZAM-moos hay-vay-ZAH NEH-sa MAH-kee-na.*

**Make sure to wipe down the equipment when you are done.**
Seque o equipamento quando terminar de usar.
*SEH-kee oo ay-kee-pa-MAIN-too KWAN-doo tayh-mee-NAH gee oo-ZAR.*

**Is there a time limit on working out here?**
Tem algum tempo limite para treinar aqui?
*tayn ahw-GOOM TAYM-poo lee-MEE-chee PAH-ra tray-NAH ah-KEE?*

**We should enter a marathon.**
A gente deveria participar de uma maratona.
*ah ZHAIN-chee day-vay-RI-a pah-chee-see-PAH gee OO-ma ma-ra-TOE-na.*

**How has your diet been going?**
Como está indo a sua dieta?
*KOE-moo ees-TAH EEN-doo ah SOO-a gee-EH-ta?*

**Are you doing keto?**
Tá fazendo a dieta cetogênica?
*tah fah-ZAIN-doo ah gee-EH-ta say-toe-ZHAY-nee-ka?*

**Make sure to stay hydrated while you work out.**
Se hidrate enquanto treina.
*see ee-DRA-chee ain-KWAN-too trayna.*

**I'll go grab you a protein shake.**
Vou pegar um shake de proteína para você.
*voe pay-GAH oom shake gee proe-tay-EE-na PAH-ra voe-SAY.*

**Do you want anything else? I'm buying.**
Quer mais alguma coisa? Eu pago.
*kehr MAH-ees ahw-GOOM-ah KOY-za? AY-oo PAH-goo.*

**I need to buy some equipment before I play that.**
Preciso comprar mais equipamentos antes de jogar.
*pray-SEE-zoo kom-PRAH MAH-ees ay-kee-pah-MAIN-toos AHN-chees gee zhoe-GAR.*

**Do you want to spar?**
Quer treinar luta?
*kehr tray-NAH LOO-ta?*

**Full contact sparring.**
Luta de contato pleno.
*LOO-ta gee kon-TA-too PLAY-noo.*

**Just a simple practice round.**
Só para treinar.
*soh PAH-ra tray-NAH.*

**Do you want to wrestle?**
Quer lutar?
*kehr loo-TAR?*

**What are the rules to play this game?**
Quais são as regras desse jogo?
*KWA-ees sawm ahs HEH-gras DAY-sy ZHOE-goo?*

**Do we need a referee?**
Precisamos de um juiz?
*pray-see-ZAM-moos gee oom zhoo-EES?*

**I don't agree with that call.**
Não concordo com essa decisão do juiz.
*NANN-oo kon-KOR-doo kom EH-sa say-see-ZAWM doo zhoo-EES.*

**Can we get another opinion on that score?**
Podemos ouvir uma segunda opinião sobre esse placar?
*po-DAY-moos oe-VEER OO-ma say-GOON-da oe-pee-nee-AWM SOE-bree AY-sy pla-KAR?*

**How about a game of table tennis?**
Vamos jogar tênis de mesa?
*VAM-moos zhoe-GAR TAY-nees gee MAY-za?*

**Do you want to team up?**
Quer formar time?
*kehr foer-MAR CHEE-me?*

**Goal!**
Gol!
*goe!*

**Homerun!**
Homerun!
*Homerun!*

**Touchdown!**
Touchdown!
*Touchdown!*

**Score!**
Ponto!
*PON-too!*

**On your mark, get set, go!**
Nos seus lugares, preparados, já!
*noos SAY-oos loo-GAH-rees, pray-pa-RAH-doos, zha!*

**Do you want to borrow my equipment?**
Quer pegar emprestado o meu equipamento?
*kehr pay-GAH ayn-prays-TAH-doo oo MAY-oo ay-kee-pah-MAIN-too?*

**Hold the game for a second.**
Pare o jogo por um momento.
*PAH-ree oo ZHOE-goo oom moe-MAIN-too.*

**I don't understand the rules of this game.**
Não estou entendendo as regras desse jogo.
*NANN-oo ees-TOE ain-tayn-DAIN-doo ahs HEH-gras DAY-sy ZHOE-goo.*

**Timeout!**
Tempo esgotado!
*TAYM-poo ays-goe-TAH-doo!*

**Can we switch sides?**
Podemos mudar de lado?
*po-DAY-moos moo-DAR gee LAH-doo?*

**There is something wrong with my equipment.**
Tem algo de errado com o meu equipamento.
*tayn AHW-goo gee ay-HA-doo kom oo MAY-oo ay-kee-pah-MAIN-too.*

**How about another game?**
Que tal outro jogo?
*kee taw OE-troo ZHOE-goo?*

**I would like a do over of that last game.**
Quero uma revanche em relação ao jogo anterior.
*KEH-roo OO-ma hay-VAN-shee ayn hay-la-SAWM AH-oo ZHOE-goo ahn-tay-REE-oh*

**Do you want to go golfing?**
Quer jogar golfe?
*kehr zhoe-GAR GOE-fee?*

**Where can we get a golf cart?**
Onde podemos pegar um carro de golfe?
*OWN-gee po-DAY-moos pay-GAH oom KAH-hoo gee GOE-fee?*

**Do you have your own club?**
Você tem seu próprio taco?
*voe-SAY tayn SAY-oo PROH-pree-oo TAH-koo?*

**Would you like to play with my spare clubs?**
Quer jogar com os meus tacos extras?
*kehr zhoe-GAR kom oos MAY-oos TAH-koos AYS-tras?*

**How many holes do you want to play?**
Com quantos buracos você quer jogar?
*KOM KWAN-toos boo-RA-koos voe-SAY kehr zhoe-GAR?*

**Do I have to be a member of this club to play?**
Preciso ser sócio do clube para jogar?
*pray-SEE-zoo sayh SOH-syo doo KLOO-bee PAH-ra zhoe-GAR?*

**Let me ice this down, it is sore.**
Deixa eu colocar um pouco de gelo, está machucado.

*DAY-sha AY-oo koe-loe-KAH oom POE-koo gee ZHAY-loo, ees-TAH mah-shoo-KAH-doo.*

**I can't keep up with you, slow down.**
Mais devagar, não estou conseguindo te acompanhar.
*MAH-ees gee-va-GAH, NANN-oo ees-TOE kon-SAY-gheen-doo ah-kom-pan-GNAR.*

**Let's pick up the pace a little bit.**
Vamos acelerar um pouco o ritmo.
*VAM-moos ah-say-lay-RAR oom POE-koo oo HEECH-moo.*

**Do you need me to help you with that?**
Precisa da minha ajuda?
*pray-SEE-za dah MEE-nya ah-ZHOO-da?*

**Am I being unfair?**
Estou sendo injusto?
*ees-TOE SAIN-doo een-ZHOOS-too?*

**Let's switch teams for the next game.**
Vamos trocar os times na próxima rodada.
*VAM-moos troe-KAH oos CHEE-mees nah PROH-see-ma hoe-DA-da.*

**Hand me those weights.**
Me dá esses pesos.
*mee dah AY-sees PAY-zoos.*

# THE FIRST 24 HOURS AFTER ARRIVING

**When did you arrive?**
Quando você chegou?
*KWAN-doo voe-SAY shay-GOE?*

**That was a very pleasant flight.**
Foi um voo muito agradável.
*foy oom voe MOON-ee-too ah-gra-DAH-vew.*

**Yes, it was a very peaceful trip. Nothing bad happened.**
Sim, foi uma viagem tranquila. Não teve nada de ruim.
*seem, foy OO-ma vy-AH-zhayn tran-KWEE-la. NANN-oo TAY-vee NAH-da gee hoo-EEN.*

**I have jetlag so need to lay down for a bit.**
Estou com jetlag, então vou precisar deitar um pouco.
*ees-TOE kom jetlag, ayn-TAWM voe pray-see-ZAR day-TAR oom POE-koo.*

**No, that was my first time flying.**
Não, é a primeira vez que eu viajo de avião.
*NANN-oo, eh ah pree-MAY-ra vays kee AY-oo vee-AH-zhoo gee ah-vee-AWM.*

**When is the check-in time?**
Qual é a hora do check-in?
*kwaw eh ah OH-ra doo check-in?*

**Do we need to get cash?**
Vamos precisar sacar dinheiro?
*VAM-moos pray-see-ZAR sah-KAR dee-GNAY-roo?*

**How much money do you have on you?**
Quanto em dinheiro você tem?
*KWAN-too ayn dee-GNAY-roo voe-SAY tayn?*

**How long do you want to stay here?**
Por quanto tempo você quer ficar aqui?
*por KWAN-too TAYM-poo voe-SAY kehr fee-KAR ah-KEE?*

**Do we have all of our luggage?**
Já pegamos toda a bagagem?
*zha pay-GA-moos TOE-da ah bah-GAH-zhayn?*

**Let's walk around the city a bit before checking in.**
Vamos dar uma olhada na cidade antes de fazer o check-in.
*VAM-moos dah OO-ma oe-LYA-da na see-DAH-gee AHN-chees gee fah-ZAYR oo check-in.*

**When is check-in time for our hotel?**
Qual é a hora do check-in no nosso hotel?
*kwaw eh ah OH-ra doo check-in noo NOH-soo oe-TEHW?*

**I'll call the landlord and let him know we landed.**
Vou ligar para o locatário e avisar que chegamos.
*voe lee-GAR PAH-ra oo loe-ka-TAH-ryo y ah-vee-ZAR kee shay-GAM-moos.*

**Let's find a place to rent a car.**
Vamos procurar um lugar para alugar um carro.
*VAM-moos proe-koo-RAR oom loo-GAR PAH-ra ah-LOO-gah oom KAH-hoo.*

**Let's walk around the hotel room and make sure it's correct.**
Vamos até o quarto do hotel pra ver se está correto.
*VAM-moos ah-TEH oo KWAR-too doo oe-TEHW prah vayh see ees-TAH koe-HEH-too.*

**We'll look at our apartment and make sure everything is in order.**
Vamos dar uma olhada no nosso apartamento e ver se está tudo em ordem.
*VAM-moos dah OO-ma oe-LYA-da noo NOH-soo ah-par-ta-MAYN-too y vayr see ees-TAH TOO-doo ayn OHR-dayn.*

# THE LAST 24 HOURS BEFORE LEAVING

**Where are the passports?**
Onde estão os passaportes?
*OWN-gee ees-TAWM oos pah-sah-POH-chees?*

**Did you fill out the customs forms?**
Você preencheu os formulários aduaneiros?
*Voe-SAY pray-ayn-SHEW oos foer-moo-LAH-ryos ah-doo-ah-NAY-roos?*

**Make sure to pack everything.**
Veja se embalou tudo.
*VAY-zha sy aim-ba-LOE TOO-doo.*

**Where are we going?**
Para onde estamos indo?
*PAH-ra OWN-gee ees-TAM-moos EEN-doo?*

**Which flight are we taking?**
Vamos pegar qual voo?
*VAM-moos pay-GAH kwaw voe?*

**Check your pockets.**
Olhe o que está nos seus bolsos.
*OH-lye oo kee ees-TAH noos SAY-oos BOE-soos.*

**I need to declare some things for customs.**
Tenho que declarar algumas coisas na aduana.
*TAYN-gnoo kee day-kla-RAR ahw-GOOM-as KOY-zas.*

**No, I have nothing to declare.**
Não, não preciso declarar nada.
*NANN-oo, NANN-oo pray-SEE-zoo day-kla-RAR NAH-da.*

**What is the checkout time?**
Qual é a hora do checkout?
*kwaw eh ah OH-ra doo checkout?*

**Make sure your phone is charged.**
Veja se o seu telefone está carregado.
*VAY-zha see oo SAY-oo tay-lay-FOE-nee ees-TAH ka-hay-GAH-doo.*

**Is there a fee attached to this?**
Tem algum custo extra?
*tayn ahw-GOOM KOOS-too AYS-tra?*

**Do we have any outstanding bills to pay?**
Ainda temos que pagar alguma conta?
*ah-EEN-da TAY-moos kee pa-GAH ahw-GOOM-ah KON-ta?*

**What time does our flight leave?**
Que horas o nosso voo sai?
*kee OH-ras oo NOH-soo voe SAH-ee?*

**What time do we need to be in the airport?**
Que horas precisamos estar no aeroporto?
*kee OH-ras pray-see-ZAM-moos ees-TAH noo ah-ay-roe-POER-too?*

**How bad is the traffic going in the direction of the airport?**
Como é o trânsito na ida para o aeroporto?
*KOE-moo eh oo TRAN-zee-too nah EE-da PAH-ra oo ah-ay-roe-POER-too?*

**Are there any detours we can take?**
Tem alguma rota alternativa que a gente possa tomar?
*tayn ahw-GOOM-ah HOH-ta ah-oo-tayh-na-CHEE-va kee ah ZHAIN-chee POH-sa toe-MAH?*

**What haven't we seen from our list since we've been down here?**
Da nossa lista, o que a gente não viu desde que chegamos?
*dah NOH-sa LEES-ta, oo kee ah ZHAIN-chee NANN-oo VEE-oo DAYS-gee kee shay-GAM-moos?*

**We should really buy some souvenirs here.**
Precisamos comprar alguns souvenirs aqui.
*pray-see-ZAM-moos kom-PRAH ahw-GOON-s soo-vay-NEES ah-KEE.*

**Do you know any shortcuts that will get us there faster?**
Você conhece algum atalho para chegar lá mais rápido?
*Voe-SAY koe-GNEH-see ahw-GOOM ah-TAH-lyo PAH-ra shay-GAH lah MAH-ees HAH-pee-doo?*

**GPS the location and save it.**
Busque a localização no GPS e salve.
*BOOS-kee ah loe-ka-lee-za-SAWM noo zhay pay EH-see y SAH-oo-vee.*

**Are the items we're bringing back allowed on the plane?**
Os itens que estamos levando são permitidos no avião?
*oos EE-tayns kee ees-TAM-moos lay-VAN-doo sawm payr-mee-CHEE-doos noo ah-vee-AWM?*

**We should call our families back home before leaving.**
Vamos ligar para a nossa família antes de partir.
*VAM-moos lee-GAR PAH-ra ah NOH-sa fa-MEE-lya AHN-chees gee pah-CHEEH.*

**Make sure the pet cage is locked.**
Veja se a caixinha do animal está trancada.
*VAY-zha sy ah kah-ee-shee-nya do ah-nee-MAHW ees-TAH tran-KA-da.*

**Go through your luggage again**
Passe a mala novamente.
*PAH-see ah MAH-la noh-va-MAYN-chee.*

# CONCLUSION

Congratulations! You have reached the end of this book and learned over **1,500** ways to express yourself in the Brazilian Portuguese language! It is a moment to celebrate, since you are now much closer to achieving complete fluency of the Brazilian Portuguese idiom.

However, the learning simply cannot end here – you may have unlocked a massive amount of incredibly useful day-to-day phrases that will get you anywhere you need to go, but are you prepared to use them correctly? Furthermore, will you actually remember them during your travels when faced with one of the situations we have presented in this book?

Only by continuously studying the material found in these chapters will you ever be able to summon the words and phrases encountered above, since it is not a matter of *what* the phrases are but *how* and *when* to use them. Knowing the exact context is crucial, as well as reinforcing your knowledge with other materials.

For this reason, we have created a quick list of tips to make the most of this Brazilian Portuguese Phrasebook and expanding your vocabulary and grasp of the Portuguese language:

1.  **Practice every day:** You can be very good at something thanks to the gift of natural talent, but practice is the only way to *stay* good. Make sure to constantly pick up the book and read the words, saying them out loud and taking note of your mistakes so you can correct them.

2.  **Read while listening:** A very popular and modern way of learning a new language is by using the RwL (reading while listening) method. It has been proven that this method can greatly boost fluency, help you ace language tests, and improve your learning in other subjects. Feel free to try out our audiobooks and other listening materials in Portuguese – you'll love them!

3. **Studying in groups:** It's always best to go on an adventure together – even if it's a language adventure! You'll enjoy yourself more if you can find someone who wants to learn with you. Look to friends, your partner, your family members, or colleagues for support, and maybe they can even help you make the process easier and quicker!

4. **Creating your own exercises:** This book provides you with plenty of material for your learning processes, and you will probably be happy with reading it every time you can...however, you need to increase the difficulty by looking for other words and phrases in the Brazilian Portuguese language which you don't know the pronunciation to and trying to decipher them for yourself. Use the knowledge you've gained with previous lessons to discover entirely new words!

With that said, we have now fully concluded this Brazilian Portuguese phrase book, which will surely accelerate your learning to new levels. Don't forget to follow every tip we have included and keep an eye out for our additional Portuguese materials.

# MORE BOOKS BY LINGO MASTERY

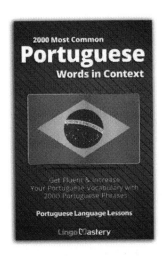

Have you been trying to learn Portuguese and simply can't find the way to expand your vocabulary?

Do your teachers recommend you boring textbooks and complicated stories that you don't really understand?

Are you looking for a way to learn the language quicker without taking shortcuts?

If you answered "Yes!" to at least one of those previous questions, then this book is for you! We've compiled the **2000 Most Common Words in Portuguese**, a list of terms that will expand your vocabulary to levels previously unseen.

Did you know that — according to an important study — learning the top two thousand (2000) most frequently used words will enable you to understand up to **84%** of all non-fiction and **86.1%** of fiction literature and **92.7%** of oral speech? Those are amazing stats, and this book will take you even further than those numbers!

**In this book:**

- A detailed introduction with tips and tricks on how to improve your learning

- A list of 2000 of the most common words in Portuguese and their translations
- An example sentence for each word – in both Portuguese and English
- Finally, a conclusion to make sure you've learned and supply you with a final list of tips

Don't look any further, we've got what you need right here!

In fact, we're ready to turn you into a Portuguese speaker... are you ready to get involved in becoming one?

**Do you know what the hardest thing for a Portuguese learner is?**

Finding PROPER reading material that they can handle...which is precisely the reason we've written this book!

Teachers love giving out tough, expert-level literature to their students, books that present many new problems to the reader and force them to search for words in a dictionary every five minutes — it's not entertaining, useful or motivating for the student at all, and many soon give up on learning at all!

In this book we have compiled 20 easy-to-read, compelling and fun stories that will allow you to expand your vocabulary and give you the tools to improve your grasp of the wonderful Portuguese tongue.

**How Portuguese Short Stories for Beginners works:**

- Each story is interesting and entertaining with realistic dialogues and day-to-day situations.
- The summaries follow a synopsis in Portuguese and in English of what you just read, both to review the lesson and for you to see if you understood what the tale was about.
- At the end of those summaries, you'll be provided with a list of the most relevant vocabulary involved in the lesson, as well as slang and sayings that you may not have understood at first glance!

183

- Finally, you'll be provided with a set of tricky questions in Portuguese, providing you with the chance to prove that you learned something in the story. Don't worry if you don't know the answer to any — we will provide them immediately after, but no cheating!
- We want you to feel comfortable while learning the tongue; after all, no language should be a barrier for you to travel around the world and expand your social circles!

So look no further! Pick up your copy of Portuguese Short Stories for Beginners and start learning Portuguese right now!

This book has been written by a native Brazilian author and is recommended for A2+ level learners.

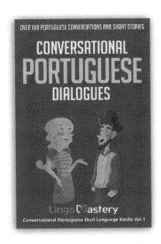

Is conversational Portuguese turning a little too tricky for you? Do you have *no idea* how to order a meal or book a room at a hotel?

If your answer to any of the previous questions was *'Yes'*, then this book is for you!

If there's even been something tougher than learning the grammar rules of a new language, it's finding the way to speak with other people in that tongue. Any student knows this — we can try our best at practicing, but you always want to avoid making embarrassing mistakes or not getting your message through correctly.

*'How do I get out of this situation?'* many students ask themselves, to no avail, but no answer is forthcoming.

Until now.

We have compiled **MORE THAN ONE HUNDRED** conversational Portuguese stories for beginners along with their translations, allowing new Portuguese speakers to have the necessary tools to begin studying how to set a meeting, rent a car or tell a doctor that they don't feel well. We're not wasting time here with conversations that don't go anywhere: if you want to know how to solve problems (while learning a ton of Portuguese along the way, obviously), this book is for you!

How Conversational Portuguese Dialogues works:

- Each new chapter will have a fresh, new story between two people who wish to solve a common, day-to-day issue that you will surely encounter in real life.

- An Portuguese version of the conversation will take place first, followed by an English translation. This ensures that you fully understood just what it was that they were saying.
- Before and after the main section of the book, we shall provide you with an introduction and conclusion that will offer you important strategies, tips and tricks to allow you to get the absolute most out of this learning material.
- That's about it! Simple, useful and incredibly helpful; you will **NOT** need another conversational Portuguese book once you have begun reading and studying this one!

We want you to feel comfortable while learning the tongue; after all, no language should be a barrier for you to travel around the world and expand your social circles!

So look no further! Pick up your copy of **Conversational Portuguese Dialogues** and start learning Portuguese *right now*!

Please notice that this book has been written with a Brazilian Portuguese touch.

Made in the USA
Columbia, SC
04 February 2023